COMING TO TERMS WITH EXPERIENCE THROUGH WRITING
Scott Oury

I make it Real by putting it into words.   *Virginia Woolf*

That was the time when words were like magic. The human mind had mysterious powers. A word spoken by chance might have strange consequences; it would suddenly come alive, and what people wanted to happen could happen–all you had to do was to say it. Nobody could explain this: That's the way it was.

> *from Shaking the Pumpkin, traditional poetry*
> *of Indian North Americas, Jerome Rothenberg*

Experience is not what happens to a [person]; it is what a [person] does with what happens to him.

> *Aldous Huxley*

Although vulnerable to error, our conversation with ourselves is our best approximation to truth.

> *Adapted from "A Voice Without a Mouth: Inner Speech,"*
> *by Denise Riley. Harpers Magazine/June 2005*

Real learning is learning how to narrate the self, how to let the self speak itself.

> *Toni Morrison*
> *Orchestra Hall, Chicago, Arts Festival speech, 11/10/90*

We are taught not to trust our own experience . . .
[but] experience is our way back home . . .

> *Terry Tempest Williams*
> *from An Unspoken Hunger*

Acknowledgements

To fully acknowledge those who have encouraged and critiqued the book-in-progress these past 34 years through dozens of drafts would fill a chapter itself. Here's a short list: Sanford Peele and Lisa Vandepaer, who listened and responded with sharp insights, hours on end, as we talked through ideas that became the first draft. Marjorie Canan, long talks and editing of a later draft. Student Cynthia Cappello, later an award-winning poet, for fine insights. Chris Hollingsworth for an extensive critique. Sally Kitt Chappell for ongoing encouragement. Gwyn Evans, Mt. Holyoke student, who presented me class after class, with attentive copyediting, a welcome surprise; and copyedited this edition of the text.

My students, who received the invitation simply to write what mattered most— and gave me a goldmine of fine, courageous writing, and the most rewarding task of figuring out just what made the writing good. Peter Elbow, leading theorist/practitioner in composition studies, who underscored the value of this "wonderful" student writing as centerpiece to the book.

Glynn Anderson, my wife, whose ongoing support, close reading of this edition, and adamant insistence (with others) that I finish the book, helped bring it to completion

Finally, Dave Champoux, of Holyoke Community College, the first teacher other than myself to use it in the classroom, presently three years running.

CONTENTS

INTRODUCTION

This book is to encourage and guide writing from experience, from life. You may have something that needs to be written, but you can't get started. Or you've started, but stopped, with questions. Am I getting it right? Is it worth anything? Do I want to pursue this? If you're writing out of experience, perhaps you've raised memories and issues that are a bit scary, even painful. In the solitary act of writing from experience, the self always surfaces, a self with uncertainties, doubts and questions, a self that matters.

But something else may be in the way as well, all too common in my teaching experience. Extensive research shows that at age three a linguistic genius takes up residence in the human brain, yours for instance. At age three, you began to use language complexly, and before long learned how to write, both for yourself and for teachers. But more and more, you were writing for teachers only. And then the grammar police arrived—from the Corrections Facility. Writing powered by your speaking voice got harnessed to correctness, lost its voice and power—and you lost your pleasure in writing.

I edited textbooks for four years and taught writing for thirty-six years, very familiar with correctness and following the rules. But early on I found that a rule-driven *attitude* toward writing stopped the flow of ideas and stifled "voice." As I changed my attitude toward correctness, students changed their attitude toward writing, and I found myself listening to voices lively, individual, and strong.

For instance, on pages 15 & 16 the voice describing an uncle's death is quite moving because the author found one rhythm for life and another for death: long sentences for ongoing life, short sentences and sentence fragments for a life cut short. On page 13 the voice describing an alcoholic mother is extremely sarcastic because the monotonous rhythm of sentences mimics mother's boring, monotonous home life. Sarcasm is then doubled: sentences that describe one mood are quickly undercut by sentence fragments describing the opposite mood, which captures the swift switch in mood classic with alcoholics.

Whether or not your "voice" has been diminished or disabled, gaining full "voice" in your writing and knowing how to use it, like a singer, is absolutely essential. This book was born in writing classes where, with early encouragement, writers soon found a "voice." The book took form as I discovered how that was happening. I was determined to help bring these writers to full voice. First, they had to find a personally invested subject. So I asked them to keep a journal/notebook of their own, and to write down *whatever came to mind with feeling*, just that: memories of recent or past happenings, random thoughts—and images of any sort, including imaginations and dreams. What came with feeling came with voice—raw, refined, soulful, sarcastic, ironic, insightful—and true.

The pleasure of voice led naturally to the pleasure of detailed description, which led to dramatic monologues, dialogues, sketches, narratives, and reflections. Exploring these descriptions for meaning led to the pleasure (sometimes pain) of discovery, and of developing meaning further with memoirs and personal essays. I structured the book using this sequence—voice to personal essay, which had developed naturally. And added a chapter on modern style.

As they wrote, these writers found a natural—modern—style of their own that cleared a path for detailed description, narration, and for thinking things through. Some of the best of these writings profusely illustrate this book.

Chapter 8 explores modern style, the cumulative sentence in particular, a style developed by outstanding writers of the past 100 years, among them, Hemingway, Faulkner, Steinbeck, Eudora Welty, and Rachel Carson.

Over the years this approach to writing has invited comments such as these.

The course has broken a major rule of writing for me–to encourage me to write in fragments and bits and pieces as they come out. Prior to this course I was not accepting of my writing if it didn't flow in full, grammatically proper sentences. Breaking that rule allows the feelings to come through foremost; the grammar, if needed, can always be added later.   *V.*

Voice. This is the first time since I have been writing in English that commas, periods, and semicolons make sense; they actually make the paper sound right to me. . . . In my previous years in American schools, I learned where I had to punctuate and it never made sense to me, so I always did it my way. I got yelled at a couple times . . . I am glad to know that after all, I wasn't wrong all the times I didn't go by the rules.   *Stela*

I had no confidence in my writing at all. I had no clue what I was doing and no one to set me straight. It is very different now. I actually like writing, and when I'm writing I don't worry the whole time I'm writing if everything is perfect. It's perfectly MY paper and that is all that matters. The less I think about screwing up the paper the more it falls into place. That is the most important thing that I've learned as a writer (that looks funny . . . me a "writer"), that it is MINE.

Jen McNabb

William Stafford, a poet and teacher of writing, writes: "Composing is done by feel rather than by rule." And when they clash, "the rule must give." Columnist William Saffire writes, "Consider the possibility that your ear may be right and the rule not a 'real rule.'"

But what happens to writing required by a college, a business, or an institution when a writer gets used to writing first by feel, attending to an emerging voice?

I remember the first couple of months. It took me a long time to write a page, which meant something. Then I began to get into being able to put my thoughts down with very little trouble. . . . Then when I began to write this term paper for health it was so damn easy writing it up it wasn't funny.

C. J.

I learned how to get my strong voice through all of my writings. I cannot conceive of my writing as I did before: something boring, useless and forced. . . . To my surprise, by the end of the semester I wrote a "quality paper," as one of my professors judged my final paper to be.

Carolina Rodriguez

The key thing I learned was to just write down whatever came to mind right then and there. That went against everything I had ever done, so I didn't think it would work. But much to my surprise, it was the best thing I did for myself as a writer.

Lori Guerra

I used to find academic writing an arduous task. I would spend hours mulling over ideas for a paper and when it came time to write the actual piece, I would sit in front of my laptop screen, glazed-eyed, experiencing writer's block. . . .

Last month, a senior friend who has edited my papers with me throughout my college career, stated: "your ideas flow much more smoothly. And, you have fewer grammatical errors in your papers . . ."

Hannah Alexander

Required writing is always a negotiation: professor/student, boss/employee. Company style/your style. It is often a difficult negotiation, even when a writer has seen what a natural writing process can do. Nancy Townsend, a returning student (Francis Perkins Scholar at Mt. Holyoke College), writes that she began her studies thinking that she "did not know how to write." Writing a paper put her "in a state of panic" (all too common), which was alleviated, she writes, by "having my college age daughters edit my papers" (uncommon, but resourceful).

But one summer she faced a "life challenge"—and turned to writing on her own.

I discovered that the words flowed from my brain to the computer keys faster than I could type. I discovered that thoughts and ideas came to my mind quickly and clearly. I discovered that writing was a great form of meditation. Writing was not hard! I had no pressures, no expectations for my writing this summer. Writing was helping me through this challenging time. Writing was helping me find the answers that I needed. I was writing for myself.

Following that elemental writing experience, she found the courage to sign up for a writing class, "excited about becoming more comfortable with writing, and no longer feeling like a deer in the headlights . . . Letting go of my fear has given me the confidence to write in a way that I never thought possible." But then her thoughts take a turn.

> *I know already that I am not as happy with this particular paper as I was with my writing this summer. But I have written this paper in a short amount of time and I do know that a college professor is going to read it. So there is a little pressure that I can't let go of and that pressure, knowing this paper will be read and analyzed, is keeping it from being better.*

As these comments attest, required writing of any sort, the academic essay also, needs this elemental process to give the mind a safe place to work, and thus give the writing life. Writing for yourself and for others should begin, and continue, with the same impulse: to let your mind find its way, on its own terms.

So where do you start? (See page vi for more detail.) First, with writing that matters. How do you get into that? Easily. Personal experience becomes the subject all but inevitably when the subject is left open. And personal experience always matters.

The best vehicle I can suggest is a notebook/journal that you can easily carry around so that any time the impulse comes—an image, memory, or thought arriving with feeling—you can write it down. Seems innocent enough, but that's where it starts.

And if little or nothing comes along?—try one of the prompts on pages 18-20, A Talk To, or A Room, two of the most successful prompts, I've discovered. Or try Freewriting, page 20, just putting pen to paper and writing *whatever* comes to mind, nonstop. Something will come along before long. Trust that.

And for guidance? For a very long time I've been a student of my students' writings. I've packed the book with these writings, for two reasons: they run a range of sophistication, so you should find them interesting but not intimidating; and the writings are from experience, lively, often dramatic, none of them written for the book, and some not even written for me. Also, students often explain their writing process as an introduction to the piece or a comment on it.

Your guides, then, will be myself and students from my entire career.

Chapter 1 examines in detail an off-the-cuff writing to see what makes it work so well. It also comments on a writing that came from having little or nothing to write about, as it turned out, a very nice piece about "nothing."

Chapter 2 explores "voice," an essential element in making your writing sound like—you.

Chapter 3 discusses description, crucial to capturing your sense of experience, and to "making sense." It also explores a few "Short Forms" that emerge naturally from description.

Chapter 4 explores the process of drawing meaning from descriptions (actual scenes and events, imaginations, and dreams), a process of discovery and surprise.

Chapters 5 and 6 extend the process of capturing experience and finding meaning with Working Essays of the Journal, and Essay/Memoir.

Chapter 7 concerns research, a natural outworking of personal essay and memoir when experience isn't quite enough to bring a writing home.

Chapter 8 explores the structure of modern writing style, phrase to sentence to paragraph to finished piece. The structure of the paragraph and groups of paragraphs is illustrated with writings from some of my favorite thinkers on writing, and constitute a very brief philosophy of writing. The chapter ends with the discussion of an academic research paper.

Chapter 9 is just a sample of the best memoir/essay writing I've gotten from students in 36 years.

Just who is this book for?

It is for writers and writers-to-be: for those who have thought that they might like to write, but haven't known how to get into it, or have been intimidated by the "correctness" machine. It is for those who have been writing, but need to revisit the elements of good writing, or find a new direction guided by a writer and teacher of writing. And (Chapter 8 especially) it is for anyone who wants an introduction to modern style, condensed and down to earth, exploring the structure of modern sentences and paragraphs.

The book is for students, but not just students, since students are not a unique human species. The book was written out of a college writing class environment, community college mostly, and Mount Holyoke College the final three years. At the community colleges where I taught, students came from a wide spectrum of society: graduates from high school; returning college students; workers in trades, technology, and professions; women raising families—and working. At Mount Holyoke College they came from a spectrum of society worldwide, several bent on changing the world. A few were English majors. They were sophisticated/not so sophisticated, cultured/not so cultured, literate/not so literate, young/not so young. Two women were in their 80s.

I imagine you fit somewhere here.

A Suggestion: to Facilitate Writing from Experience

Get a notebook/journal you can easily carry with you. When you have—or can make—a little space and time, begin by writing, perhaps randomly, what captures your attention with special feeling or a sense of importance: a scene, a person, an object, an event, a memory, an imagination, a dream.

Think of this notebook/journal as yours alone, to keep, perhaps to share. But the prime value—always—is in the act of writing.

Don't let thoughts of length define the writing; short is fine; long is fine. Let any entry call its length; when it feels as if it's over, it's over, for now. Think of a song. If you find that you need some starters, try any of the suggested descriptions and imaginations, pages 18-21. These have proved surprising—and revealing.

With this notebook/journal *don't* keep a simple diary or log of daily events. Focus on *one* significant object, person, event, or scene. The subject will expand; depend on it.

Begin writing as if you were talking, so that your "voice" captures the feel of what you're writing, its rhythm, accent, pace, tone, and intensity. (I'll talk about "voice" in Chapter 2.) As you write, get into your *senses,* the sensuous specifics of your experience, actual or imagined. Bring yourself into the *moments* of the experience, one by one. That's essential. As you capture the sense of an experience, the experience will become more real, alive, presenting unexpected aspects and insights. (See Chapter 3 for description.)

A suggestion for your notebook/journal: *do your first writings* on the *right-hand page. Leave the left-hand page blank* so that you can return to those first writings, think about them, perhaps add to them, and develop their meanings. Without turning a page you can quickly glance at your first writings *as* you think and write about them. This is commonly called a "double entry notebook." (Does this have a managerial ring? It's an invitation.)

Why a notebook/journal? To limber up your writing muscles in the absence of pressure to perform, to avoid tension, to let yourself walk or run at your own pace, and to see what happens. A journal lets you write extensively, apparently at random; but that apparent randomness gives your mind—on its own—freedom to explore a circumstance or subject at length. "On its own," that must sound strange; but it is common for journals to work through a subject without the author's full awareness, sometimes with little or no awareness at all. The mind *constantly* explores, essays, what matters most in our experience. A notebook/journal invites the mind to give it form.

Writers of all sorts have used notebooks and journals to give themselves space and time to get it down before they have to get it right. Sometimes, as Virginia Woolf writes, those in-the-moment journal writings get it right.

Personal Note: an Attitude and a Style

Correctness and grading for correctness are pervasive in almost any environment associated with schooling—and beyond, even game shows. You get grades, A to F, depending on your percentage of rights, in school and out of school.

With any craft or discipline, essential elements need to be learned and practiced (perhaps evaluated) until they're right. I have plenty to say in this book about elements essential to punctuation and grammar, but with a difference: Punctuation and grammar must serve "voice," help bring to full meaning the words, phrases, and sentences emerging.

Throughout the book you will hear an *encouraging* voice, intent on bringing your own voice into print. I have enjoyed teaching, immensely, loved the exchange with students, laughter more than occasionally erupting in my classes. I hope to have brought my enjoyment of teaching into the book, humor included. Coming to terms with experience can be exacting and serious, yet filled with the multiple pleasures and delight writers for ages have found.

1 BEGINNING IN THE PRESENT–YOURS

The mind spends most of its time making sense of our lives–with great intelligence and sophistication, mostly without our awareness. That's a prime reason to begin writing simply what your mind offers, so that you expand awareness of your ongoing life—and intelligence.

The mind constantly makes sense of our lives—what does that mean? What good is it to capture that sense in writing? The following writing came from an evening's writing exercise. Reading from a list of qualities attached to each of the senses, I encouraged a group of writers to pick up on whatever struck them. Camille, author of the following piece, heard, "you're smelling something foul," bent her head, and wrote in a white heat for 40 minutes, picking up additional sense-attached words as she wrote.

Excrement somewhat like that of an infant's–gross ammonia fills the room, reminds me of diapers, dead <u>flesh</u>! This is the stench I smell; however it is in reality living flesh, mildewed with age, dry and flaky. Somewhere in the distant air I smell the faint fragrance of blended medications . . . my stomach starts to turn as my brain finally realizes and gets in tune with the situation. I feel like I am in hell, helpless, but yet full of pity for in reality I am on the second floor in a small offset room in a nursing home.

Yes, sad but true to be so sick and old and be so mistreated. I worked in a nursing home as an aide for two months wanting to conquer the world and make them all a better place. But to my disappointment, found it a challenge beyond my control. Tears were streaming down my face as I walked off my ward for the final time. The only recognition I have in myself is knowing maybe for those two, short months I made some people happy. It's just that psychologically I couldn't bear it any longer.

Ya know, I'm really pissed at you [the instructor]; that was a part of my life nearly a year ago, something I am trying to block out and it comes back to haunt me once again. God help me to forget that horrible part of my past; why won't someone help them? And shit, don't say report them cause it don't work.

That's it, you asked for it; I am not gonna stop now. Sight, is that what you want to read about? Well you're not gonna get pretty colors; I like blue or yellow and orange. You're gonna get <u>Black</u> and <u>grey</u> and soot and disgust.

Ninety-pound people who are wrinkled with age, lying on their sides and perhaps half off the bed, in that position for hours and sometimes days.

Some of them weeping softly to themselves, others lying with such apathy. I am full of disgust. Lethargic and weak, fearing everyone they meet. My stomach just churns.

. . . they have holes in their skin, raw and tender from lying in one position for so long. Bumps and swelling on their heads and knees from falling on the floor and being left to bleed. That's it, no more!

I don't know, I can't help it; that's the first time I have expressed my hatred for this, so I must get it all out. A <u>cube</u>, is that what you want next? OK, a square room with some square, bed-square, windows; square dressers with square drawers. That's all these people ever saw. With square walls. Exciting life, isn't it—with caretakers just as square as the walls.

No more, I'm really burning out; I've told people but never written it. Well that so-called ton of bricks flowed off like matchsticks.

I

Really Feel

Good.

Camille D.

What does it mean for Camille to make sense? A double meaning is suggested: 1. her mind spotlights features that hit the senses: excrement, gross ammonia, diapers, black and grey, wrinkled with age, weeping, and square, square, square; 2. as her sense of the situation becomes more complete, she understands it more fully, "*makes* sense" of it. So "making sense" involves both getting the feel, taste, scent, sound, and sight of a situation, and understanding in human terms what these senses mean.

What good is making sense of this situation for Camille? Capturing her sense of the nursing home, she comes to terms with it, so much so that she can let it go for good, something she hadn't been able to do for a year. And, as it turned out, she was able to follow a career in nursing. (No small thing, given her experience of the nursing home.)

But what makes it so important to get the *full* sense of a situation? Couldn't Camille have summed it up in a paragraph or two? Summing it up is exactly what she does in paragraphs two and three. But it doesn't work, the summing up, the generalities: "[I] found it a situation beyond my control. . . . I couldn't bear it any longer." She said such things to her friends for a year.

So there's a point to be made that underlies much of the writing that I'll encourage and discuss; it involves a pun: To make sense, you need to capture a situation in terms of your five senses, all the particulars with which your mind has been impressed. Making general statements only won't "make sense." (You will hear this again.)

Camille first gets the **smell** of this nursing home. It smells like crap in the diapers of a helpless baby. It smells like dead flesh, or living flesh mildewed with age.

Smell comes first, not surprisingly, since the sense of smell reaches our emotions immediately. Why recall the experience of a nursing home first by the smell of excrement? It's a shitty situation. (The metaphor is perfect.) The old people are literally, and in effect, lying in it, like babies, helpless, and left to dry up and die.

She's got the smell of it.

Next she picks up on **color** and fills out that sense of the situation: "You're not gonna get pretty colors; I like blue or yellow and orange. You're gonna get Black and grey and soot and disgust." That makes sense; it's a black situation, death-like, hopeless. And grey, depressing. And, like soot, nearly impossible to clean up.

Next she gives herself very powerful **visual and aural images.**

> . . . *people wrinkled with age, lying on their sides and perhaps half off the bed, in that position for hours and sometimes days. Some of them weeping softly to themselves, others lying with such apathy.*

She can hardly stand what she has recreated, the total neglect of the residents, their suffering and fear. She is "full of disgust," her "stomach just churns." She will have "no more" of it.

But she must continue; some inner vitality is urging her to a complete sense of the situation—and to let it go for good.

> *O. K., a square room with some square, bed-square windows; square dressers with square drawers. That's all these people ever saw. With square walls. Exciting life, isn't it—with caretakers just as square as the walls.*

With her sense of its **structure (square)**, comes an inescapable conclusion: There's no way out, not even a view of a happier world outside. Through "bed-square windows" the view is not of the world outside, but (metaphorically) only of their bed-ridden condition. *Everything* is square; this "horrible" situation is fixed, permanent. She cannot possibly change it; she can let it go.

Camille (along with the writers you have read and will read) took liberties: to write naturally, to write with feeling, to choose her subject, and to "break the rules." Camille's writing benefits just because she takes liberties. She feels free to swear and to use street language. "And shit, don't say report them because it don't work." "You're gonna . . ." (twice). But it is just this angry, street voice that captures her anger.

3

She uses sentence fragments:

Ninety-pound people who are wrinkled with age, lying on their sides and perhaps half off the bed, in that position for hours and sometimes days. Some of them weeping softly to themselves, others lying with such apathy. I am full of disgust. Lethargic and weak, fearing everyone they meet. My stomach just churns.
. . . they have holes in their skin, raw and tender from lying in one position for so long. Bumps and swelling on their heads and knees from falling on the floor and being left to bleed. That's it, no more!

All but two sentences in the first paragraph are fragments; one in the second is a fragment. But it is in these two paragraphs–and with just these fragments–that the writing peaks, powerfully capturing the residents' neglect and suffering. Sentence fragments, ask any professional writer, are useful, sometimes necessary. Listen to what happens when the sentences are made grammatically correct.

I'm seeing ninety-pound people who are wrinkled with age. They're lying on their sides and perhaps half off the bed. They've been in that position for hours and sometimes days. Some of them are weeping softly to themselves; others are lying with such apathy.

The guts of the writing are gone with the revision to complete sentences.

Camille feels free to accept what her mind offered. The subject is personal, and painful. But there it is, demanding to be fully explored. She goes with it. In the process she gets more than she wanted.

This cuts several ways. She gets more pain than she wanted, more awareness than she wanted, but more satisfaction than she ever expected. She feels good, really good. She has taken this "horrible" situation by the throat.

That's the pattern. The author translates tough situations to *her* terms—and comes to terms with the experience. And if you've raised intense personal stuff—you've got options: give it a fictional, third-person character: deal with the matter more broadly as an issue; or research to gain knowledge beyond your own experience.

But at times you may think that you have little or nothing to write, at least nothing as dramatic as some of the writings you'll be reading. In the following piece the author writes about his best, well, non-writing experience.

My Best Writing Experience
I don't have a long story to tell about my wonderful writing experiences. To tell the truth I don't write much at all. I am a lefty and according to my wife I "write really screwed up." I have taken notes for school and when I was in the

4

army, but for the most part I avoid writing. I guess with that in mind I would have to say that "my best writing experience" is the simple yet profound act of signing my name. My signature is not something I gave any thought to until I was an adult. Most of the time not even then. But once I sign my name on a paycheck, I can do all sorts of things. I can help support my family, I can spend the weekend playing miniature golf with my children, I can surprise my wife with flowers that she never expected. I can watch my favorite shows on an almost-paid-for television. With every signature on a paycheck I come closer to owning the 30 minute image of Dave Barry on a 27" Zenith.

With barely one stroke of the pen I can repay people who have trusted me with credit. Something that at one point in life I never would have imagined. Knowing that businesses trust my signature, two words and an initial, gives me a sense of pride and accomplishment.

The fact that sometimes my signature isn't even legible doesn't seem to bother the people who loan me money or take my credit cards. This is not to say that I sign my name illegibly on purpose, I don't. It's just that sometimes I forget the power it holds; legible or not, I can sign a mortgage paper on a house for my family, one with separate bedrooms for my boys, so the older one doesn't wake up the little one every morning at 5:00 a.m.

My signature on all sorts of documents can make the difference between a comfortable life or a hard life. It can make certain that after my death my family is taken care of. Signing my name on things gives me independence and at the same time ties me to three or four department stores, a Mobil gas station, and a better part of Toys 'R' Us. How one small piece of writing can make such an impact, create such affluence, demand attention and wield so much power is truly amazing.

I suppose that in some small way before now I must have given thought to my signature because when my first son was born I made sure that when he was older he would be signing the same name.

R. H. Pac

A signature doesn't seem too promising as a subject. But notice how Pac teases out his subject; he can do all sorts of things with his signature. With his signature he finds himself trusted. It doesn't even have to be legible to be powerful. It gives him and his family a comfortable life, and makes sure that his family will be taken care of when he's not there any longer.

Paragraph by paragraph he draws out the implications of "signature." And he has some fun with the usual expectations about writing: that writing should be "wonderful," that it must be complex and long, that it has to be legible, and that it must be preceded by considerable thought. He plays with his subject, and in the process produces a pleasurable piece, with a few insights.

Notice anything common to both of the previous writings (different as they are)? Each has its own *distinctive* feel and character, its own tone and mood. Each writing begins with a particular quality of voice that follows a course of feeling and comes to completion, like a song. Call it "theme." Keep that in mind as you write; sing it through.

PS: On Fragments: Sentence fragments—in spite of their use in professional writing—are widely prohibited in classrooms, by writing handbooks, and (you can't miss it) the "Word" grammar check. But read The New York Times, The Chicago Tribune, Harpers, The Atlantic Monthly, The New Yorker, some of the best writing in the country: fragments are used as necessary—for emphasis. The rest of us, supposedly, can use fragments only if we *know* that we are "breaking the rules," and know *how* to break them.

But, a simple principle holds for the use of fragments, nicely explained in John Dawkins' article [in College Composition and Communication 46/December 1995, p. 535]: ". . . a clause is independent [a complete sentence] if the missing element can be readily provided by a native speaker." That is, if the subject or verb of a sentence fragment is understood, we read the fragment as a complete sentence, as if the subject or verb were actually there. Sentence fragments are OK. Useful. (With a little green underline Word's grammar check brings the last sentence fragment to my attention.) Professional writers use them as they wish. So should we.

PPS: On Subject Matter: Over 40 years of observing the writing process with the subject left open, I find that subjects that *matter* inevitably result, right off. Often that involves the impact of experience present or past, sometimes strong, sometimes painful. Writers have often shared with me their double response: I don't want to write about this—I want to write about this. "Want to" almost always wins; a vital urge trumps. And for you, dear reader-writer, I will urge simply that you allow your strongest impulses to call your subject, and promise that you will have a subject—that matters. And that you will be up to it.

2 VOICE

Voice, I think, shows the heart of the person writing.   *Ryan Braastad*

Voice is the process of giving the gift of ourselves to the reader.

Peter McGrady

*I liked my "Room" piece. Wow, I rarely ever say that about my writings.
Why? Well, I guess because it came from the heart. I wrote like I speak. I have
never done that before. With most of my English papers I am so fed up with
writing those "big words" that make a paper sound more sophisticated, that I
never really concentrated on what I was actually writing.*

A. Partyka

Grammar or rules of construction should not strangle the voice in your writing.

Eunji

*Writing this first (voice) piece showed me that I could put punch in my writing
(without getting in trouble).*

Dianna

*I like the way that the writers [in this book] are able to use tempo and lists
and various marks of punctuation to convey a certain mood or movement or
feeling. It is as if the flow of the writing is mimicking the actions being written
about.*

William K.

*I really like that little entry because it displays the exact way my mind was
thinking . . .*

Kevin Bouvier

Take care of the sounds and the sense will take care of itself   *Lewis Carol.*

7

. . . the sense of every meaning has a particular sound which each individual is instinctively familiar with . . .
All that can save [sentences] is the speaking tone of voice somehow entangled in the words and fastened to the page for the ear of the imagination. That is all that can save poetry from sing-song, all that can save prose from itself.

Robert Frost

As a writer, even as a child, long before what I wrote began to be published, I developed a sense that meaning itself was resident in the rhythms of words and sentences and paragraphs . . .

Joan Didion

. . . the sound [the writer's] words make on paper.   *E. B. White, on style*

"Voice," is central to writing. Voice conveys what is happening moment by moment in the mind of the writer, a mind not quite like anyone else's, working with experiences not quite like anyone else's. Unique. "Voice" conveys a writer's unique response to experience.

Note some of the features of "voice." (Think of someone speaking.)

- Tone
- Pitch: high or low
- Intensity: loud or soft
- Pace: fast or slow, smooth or choppy
- Rhythm and accent
- The use of words and phrases that come with a *particular* tone: so? so what, get real, oh, face it, you don't say, *really,* really?
- The use of words that mimic particular sense impressions: slap, murmur, tickle, bubble, slice, crash, soft, tiny, gigantic, awesome.

These features of "voice" give an intimate, human sense to writing.

"That's it, you asked for it; I am not gonna stop now. Sight, is that what you want to read about? Well you're not gonna get pretty colors; I like blue or yellow and orange. You're gonna get <u>Black</u> and <u>grey</u> and soot and disgust.

8

Remember Camille's street voice? She's challenging her instructor, and voicing naked anger at the nursing home. Notice the pace of the short, to-the-point sentences, and the accents and intensity of the last sentence: ". . . <u>Black</u> and <u>grey</u> and soot and disgust." Just the multiple use of "and" intensifies and accents the sentence; the capital B and underlining, give it further accent.

Notice the change in voice when she in effect opens the door to the residents.

> *Ninety-pound people who are wrinkled with age, lying on their sides and perhaps half off the bed, in that position for hours and sometimes days. Some of them weeping softly to themselves, others lying with such apathy. I am full of disgust.*

It's a poignant, sympathetic voice that describes the residents, using only sentence fragments, as if she could only point—there. As if, at first, she couldn't *say* anything. But notice the impact of the short statement that follows the fragments: "I am full of disgust."

She would have ruined that impact just by lengthening the sentence a little: "This situation fills me with disgust." Instead she listens to the character of her disgust. She repeats the pattern: "Lethargic and weak, fearing everyone they meet. My stomach just churns."

These paragraphs have a telling rhythm: poignant observations—short statement; poignant observations—short statement.

In the following piece a young woman discusses the lack of attention she got as a girl from her father—and what she did about it. Notice the qualities of voice that bring this across: the pace and accent of short sentence fragments.

> *One day I was bored and I noticed my Dad playing catch with the boys a couple of doors down. From that moment on I was no longer a girl. Cut my hair short—so short. Got on my Levis and high tops. No shirt. God, I went out with no shirt. And played ball. Climbed trees. Broke windows. Played on the tracks. Joined an all boys baseball team.*
>
> H.

Once she decides that she must be a boy, the piece begins to move.   Short sentence fragments kick up the pace, as if she were saying, "Ok, if that's what it takes—out of my way."

That pace is easy to ruin by making statements of these fragments, and combining some of them so that they flow.

> *I cut my hair short—so short, and got on my Levis and high tops, but no shirt. God, I went out with no shirt. And I played ball, climbed trees, broke windows, played on the tracks, and joined an all-boys baseball team.*

9

This kills the pace and the accent of her action. Not only that, reducing each of the sentence fragments to phrases *de-emphasizes* these actions. In her original, each action is given the emphasis of a sentence. Only one statement interrupts the sequence of sentence fragments: "God, I went out in no shirt." That unusual action is given just the emphasis it needs, as a statement. Did she plan all this? I doubt it. She got the feel of it.

What gives the next writing its "voice?"

Imaginary hands holding me down. Again, anger—tremendous struggle, resentment. Don't feel meek—feel like Samson—huge, in a rage—breaking bonds.

J. M. P.

Cramped sentences. Cramped experience. Notice how punctuation, and the use of sentence fragments, restricts the movement. She is being "held down"; so are the sentences, by commas—and dashes. She can't move; the sentences can't move.

The following description concerns a mother's observation of her daughter getting ready to go out for the night. Notice the pace.

We've chatted all through her cleaning and fluffing and the last information I receive as this beautiful woman walks out the door impeccably attired is a quick run-down as to what I should tell to whomever calls for her on the phone while she is gone.

Jackie N.

Here's a run-on sentence if you've ever seen one, but it imitates run-on, nonstop movements, the pace of a daughter's preparations.

Rhythm and accent closely relate to pace. Following is the description of the hand-lashing an eight-year old received for sassing her father, as she wrote with some irony, "once too often."

So he made me <u>stand</u> there while he slapped me across the face. With his palm, then his back hand–"I'm sorry." With his palm then his back hand—I yelled, "I'm sorry I'm sorry!!" (And I really was.)

Karen M.

This is the exact rhythm and accent of the beating, and of her response: palm/back hand . . . palm/back hand: four slaps. "I'm sorry I'm sorry," carries a clear sense of the rapidity of her response. Suppose she had written: "He slapped

10

me with his palm, then his back hand. I said, 'I'm sorry.' He slapped me again with his palm then his backhand. I yelled, "I'm sorry, I'm sorry." Rhythm and accent disappear in the rewrite.

"<u>Stand</u>," in the first sentence has a special accent just because it's underlined. Karen uses the parentheses in the last sentence to show a change in voice, a comment aside.

Look at rhythm and accent again. The paragraph that follows is from a description of a family gathering in a Greek household. Two kids have been wanting to try Metaxa on the sly. "The Greek," patriarch of the household, catches the girl—and gives her a shot to drink in one gulp. She swallows, her throat burns, she chokes, gasps—the gathering erupts.

> *The Greek howls with laughter, roars till tears come down his face, till he's choking on cigar smoke, till the whole damned table is laughing with him, pounding fists, hands, bottles, laughing and laughing; and I'm laughing right with them.*
>
> *Eileen Flynn*

With her long sentence Eileen catches the rhythm of the eruption in progress. "Howls" and "roars" take obvious accents, as do "fists, hands, bottles" and "laughing and laughing."

Rhythm at root is repetition, the ancient device of repeating elements that are similar or the same. It's as old as drumbeats and chants.

In the following piece the repetitions are quite plain. (I'll show by indenting.)

Feelings from my childhood start to surface.
> *Feelings I've successfully suppressed for twenty years.*
> *Feelings that I have convinced myself didn't exist.*
>> *The emptiness of a house where four people live but no family life exists.*
>> *No communication.*
>> *No sharing.*
>> *No caring*
>>> *A mother who works to get away from a life she hates.*
>>> *A father who shows no feelings--no emotion. Never has anything to say.*
>>> *A brother who bums around and gets in trouble with the police.*
>>>
>>> *Jill*

11

The rhythm and accent in Jill's piece are obvious in the repetition of the same or similar words: feelings, no, mother, father, brother. Repetition not only makes for rhythm and accent; each repetition raises the pitch and intensity. Emotion builds in this piece. Repetition always builds intensity. Listen to the beat.

She makes just one statement at start; the rest are sentence fragments. What if she had made complete statements of each fragment?

> *Feelings from my childhood start to surface. I've successfully suppressed them for twenty years, convincing myself that they didn't exist. The house felt empty, the kind of emptiness where four people live but no family life exists. . . .*

With the rewrite, the accent, tone and intensity of the experience have faded.

Look again at the pattern of repetition, the end of a personal essay. (Again, I'll indent.)

> *I have discovered an important tool–courage.*
> *Courage to face life head on;*
> *courage to face adversities and realize that*
> *life is more than a trial; it is an adventure.*
> *Life is not dreary; it is exciting.*
> *Life is not all sorrows; it is joy.*
> *Life is not worthless; it is precious.*
>
>

E. M. B.

It's not difficult to feel her passion, partly by the structure she uses, but in good part by her use of repetition. Parallel contrasts, "life is not/it is," heighten the emphasis.

This next entry exhibits a quality of "voice" not yet emphasized, words and phrases that embody a particular tone of voice.

> *How dare you keep waltzing in here as if you own the place yet? As if you own us yet? Don't you know you gave that up in the divorce decree? What did you think? Did you think you could get it on _paper_ that you are no longer responsible for me—or the kids—or the house mortgage—or the utilities—or the past bills . . . and _then_ think you could just open that front door and blast in, "Daddy's Home" style? Get real! Face it! If you haven't wanted us as a burden to you for the last 8 years, as you've demonstrated—why—why would you want us now?*
>
> *Now that the hassles have been taken away you want to reclaim "us"—reclaim your domain? Have your cake and eat it too?*
>
> *I don't think so! In all the 15 years we've been here I've done more work fixing the house than you ever have. _I_ painted, peeled, plastered, hammered,*

nailed, sawed, mowed, trimmed, weeded, improvised, bought odds and ends, fixed door handles, appliances, kids bikes, etc. etc. This is my domain!

K. B.

Quite a few words and phrases carry a certain tone of voice: "Get real!" "Face it!" "I don't think so." Notice other devices of "voice" she uses: repetitions, dashes, exclamation and question marks, all deftly managing voice. Take a good look at the hammering accent of the long list, next to last sentence. And following it, the short final sentence. Is this is her domain? I guess.

In the long journal entry out of which this next paragraph is taken, the writer has been describing her family background, particularly her alcoholic parents. Discussion of her father, a member of AA, precedes this paragraph.

My mother is an alcoholic who is <u>not</u> a member of AA. She doesn't work. Mother sits at home and cleans, and cooks, and rots. And bitches, and bitches, and bitches. Mother hates herself. Mother hates everything. Except when she gets plowed. Then mother loves everyone and everything. Except herself. "Why don't you love me?" says mother. " I love you! WHY DON'T YOU LOVE ME?!"

M. M.

Notice that most of the sentences are short, to the point, angry. Observe that the commas slow the "cleans, and cooks," and "bitches and bitches" sentences to a terrible monotony, and add disgust to the anger. And the period after "rots"—lets rot last a bit longer.

Her anger grows with mother's quick switch in behavior, which she captures perfectly. Mother is one way when she is drunk. Another sober. The short, contrary sentences alternating with sentence fragments capture that well. "Mother hates herself. Mother hates everything. Except when she gets plowed. Then mother loves everyone and everything. Except herself." The fragments, beginning with "Except," capture mother's quick switch of attitude just because they are sentence fragments, slipped in quickly.

Let's make the fragments into complete statements: "But when she gets plowed, mother loves everyone and everything except herself." The quick switch is lost.

Here's another entry that uses these devices of voice, and others less obvious.

A ten year old Girl Scout came to my door recently. She just walked right in. She held out her hand and said, "six bucks." As natural as could be. No hesitation. "Six bucks," she said again. I never saw her before. Didn't order any cookies either. She just kept her hand out. "Six bucks." I gave her the money. I had to. She had the cookies. I had to pay her. No choice in the

13

matter. The cookies were there. Her hand was held out. What could I do? I didn't order any cookies. I paid her. What else could I do? What if I had refused? Her den mother could have come over and foreclosed on my soul. Den mothers can do that.

She took the money. Did a 180 degree turn, and left. But she didn't leave. She plopped down on my porch. Took inventory of her cookie wagon. Counted her ill-gotten gain. She had more loot than I've had in a long time. She sat awhile, then cast off in search of more unsuspecting souls. You can't say no to a Girl Scout. I got off lucky. I still have my porch. I'll never answer the door again.

Brad J.

The short sentences describe the event, action by action, without explanation, and seem quite appropriate to a Girl Scout's actions: short and simple, just give me the money. These actions alternate with the writer's thoughts exactly as they occur.

"Six bucks." As natural as could be. No hesitation. "Six bucks," she said again. I never saw her before. Didn't order any cookies either. She just kept her hand out. "Six bucks." I gave her the money. I had to . . .

Brad's voice matches the experience: her short demand; his thoughts, incredulous, tumbling one after another; her demand repeated; his disbelief: this can't be–how could this be–happening.

Look at the short sentences, some of them fragments, that describe how she makes off with the money.

She took the money. Did a 180 degree turn, and left. But she didn't leave. She plopped down on my porch. Took inventory of her cookie wagon. Counted her ill-gotten gain.

Each action, taking the money, turning, leaving, plopping down on the porch, is separate and brief, just like his series of short statements and fragments. Notice the sound of "plopped down on my porch." Substitute "sat down on my porch." (She's gained 20 pounds.)

Notice the tone of words he has chosen to describe her money, her actions, and her victims: "ill gotten gain," "loot," "cast off," "unsuspecting souls." She's corrupt, a thief, and a pirate preying on the innocent, all presented with humor. The words "foreclosed on my soul" also carry humor in the overstatement, as does his comment, "I got off lucky. I still have my porch." A humorous tone runs all through the entry.

Observe again that the subject calls for a voice like this. Girl Scout selling cookies meets unsuspecting customer—it's a laugh. Brad makes the most of it.

14

I've got to make a qualification concerning the match of "voice" with subject content: *What* is being said plays its own part in "voice." Content constantly tells voice what's going on. Content provides the cue; voice takes it from there. Content is the body; voice, the legs that put the body in motion.

Essays relying mainly on explanation and argument must also have "voice" to give life to their ideas and to bring the point home. Following is the end of an eight-page essay on the changes made to an Alzheimer's unit for veterans, bad changes made, without consideration, by the new administration. Throughout the essay Sandy, the author, clearly narrates these mindless changes with an ironic voice driven by long experience.

> *Whose best interest is being served here? The interests of these brave men who served our country and are now locked away from the outside world for their own safety with bare walls to look at, or those of the "team" who sit in their offices in the "executive suite" and make decisions "by the book" for people that they do not personally know and will never take the time to know.*
>
> *In our lives, none of the things that are part of normal living for the Alzheimer victim would be acceptable to us. All the more reason for all of us who work in this field to do anything and everything possible to make the lives of these men, who fought for and risked their lives for us, as happy and comfortable and productive as we can.*
>
> *Sandy*

With the question and following long sentence fragment, Sandy's outrage shows. "Locked away," and "bare walls" sharply characterize the veterans' situation. She sardonically contrasts their plight with those in the "executive suite" making decisions "by the book" for those they "do not personally know and will never take the time to know." She emphasizes the exec's lack of personal knowledge with this repetition: they don't know the veterans and "will never take the time to know them."

In the last paragraph her voice changes to a plea for those in the field to do "anything and everything" (note the repetition and accent) to help these veterans, and make their lives "as happy and comfortable and productive as we can" (notice the three beats, emphasized with the use of "and").

In this final entry the subject is death, a life cut short. Content informs its voice unmistakably. Observe how the sentences match ongoing life—and life cut short.

> *I didn't finish the book; I'm very tired of death. It's Sunday night, late, and I can't sleep. I got the news today that my uncle died. He had cancer. He was only fifty.*

15

Why are we born–if only to die? Is that the price we pay for being a higher animal, that we know someday we'll be gone? When we die, life will keep on going like we were never here at all. Are we? What is it for?

Uncle Ed was just an ordinary person like anybody else. They told him about the cancer in September and nobody could believe it. Every day since was a steady downhill progression, and when I saw him last Tuesday I hardly knew him.

What do you say? Is it a blessing? Would he rather live with the pain and the people he loved or give it all up–nobody asked him. He had no choice.

Never–never will he see his kids smile or feel his wife's arms around him or complain about the weather or taxes or see birds flying or hear a little voice call "grandpa."

[Elisabeth Kubler] Ross said in her book that when somebody dies the survivors feel a loss of that person, but what about that person who for months had to get used to the thought of losing everything. Everything.

I can't handle it–I'm crying now and I'm mad and hurt and scared—when is it my turn?

When my father died my mother said he was going away on a business trip. He's never coming home.

D. J.

Paragraph by paragraph the tone and rhythm of this piece match comments and questions weighing life and death. (The subject asks for a voice like this.) In the first paragraph short, terse statements say: I'm tired of being faced with death. Then two very short sentences suggest its finality: "He had cancer. He was only fifty." Life is cut short; so are the sentences.

Out of this tone, questions and comments about life rise in long, unbroken sentences, sentences like an ongoing life. But these are begun, or brought to conclusion, by short sentences or phrases on death—like death. Life brought up short.

When we die, life will keep on going like we were never here at all. Are we? What is it for?

What do you say? Is it a blessing? Would he rather live with the pain and the people he loved or give it all up—nobody asked him. He had no choice.

Never—a never will he see his kids smile or feel his wife's arms around him or complain about the weather or taxes or see birds flying or hear a little voice call "grandpa."

Observe how sharply "Never–never. . ." with just a dash, sets the finality of death against the long, unbroken sentence describing ongoing life. And later, how

16

". . . everything. <u>Everything</u>." with its repetition, underscoring, and one-word sentence, brings this sequence to its end. Finally the author reflects upon her own life and her father's death. The characteristic rhythm is completed: one long sentence for the "business trip", one short, for "never coming home."

Thoughts on life and death are deftly voiced in this entry.

Different voices speak through each of those entries. In each, an individual confronts a unique experience and says what is felt and thought. Some of these entries are journal writings, little changed, voice emerging naturally.

Encourage voice in your writing. You will find that your writings sound more like—you.

However, first writings may not always voice themselves so easily and so well. You may have to work with your voice to get it to sound right. Listen. Be attentive to the talk developing in your head. Put commas in for small pauses; put semicolons in for longer pauses in complex sentences, or between closely related statements (as in this sentence). Use periods for a full stop, a drop in the voice. Use an exclamation mark for a dramatic statement! Dashes—for emphasis—or a break in thought. Parentheses (if you wish) to de-emphasize, or to drop into another voice. Punctuation can be finely managed, in part, just by listening to your "voice." (See the Appendix on Punctuation for more detailed suggestions.)

Especially, and always, trust the course that your feelings take. Draw out your feeling; let them run their *full* course, as if they were a song finding its way home. Your writing will reach resolution and conclusion as you voice a full course of feelings and exhaust them. In the process a theme will emerge.

PS—Dramatic Writings: Are you feeling that you won't be able to write the kind of dramatic pieces that you've been reading and are likely to read? Drama isn't necessary, just your voice coming through, whatever the subject, *fitting* the subject. Not to worry; drama will be there when it's needed.

Some Terms Defined: Before the chapter on description, a word on some terms used. **Description** is commonly used for writing that captures the sense of experience, whether of an object, person, scene, or event. **Narration** is used to describe only an event (a happening or series of happenings). But it's cumbersome to use **description and narration** to cover everything from objects to events. So I'll often use the term **description** to cover both. But if *events* are of *primary* concern, I'll use **narration, or narrative, or story.**

Image is often used generically as a term to cover everything from "mental images" (of the five senses), images in your head, to images that are committed to paper: "descriptions and narrations." So I'll use **image** as an all-purpose, generic term to cover the sense of sight, sound, touch, taste and smell, whether in your head or described on paper.

17

Descriptions and Imaginations to Try

Attempt the following descriptions and imaginations at various times when you're in the mood or when you feel lost for writings. Think of them as symbolic frames for your mind to fill.

As you write, glance at the bulleted items. If one (or more) raises a strong image—incorporate it in your description. If not, ignore the bulleted item. Your journal is probably a good place for these at start; but often, these descriptions raise subjects that can be explored at length.

A TALK TO (a "dramatic monologue"): Recall or imagine someone for whom you have strong feelings, negative or positive. Imagine them in a particular place. Describe place and person. Talk to them, or give them a "talking to." Don't let them talk—but describe their *physical* responses to the talk.

Make a new paragraph when you describe their physical responses, and again when you return to your talk. And put your own talk, your words, in quotes. Make the talk *happen* in one particular place and at one particular time. That's crucial. Not, "sometimes," "most of the time," "I could," "he would." Make it *happen* in the moment, moment by moment; give yourself the *experience.*

BREATH AND HEARTBEAT: Focus on your breathing, the stream of air flowing in to fill your lungs, then out again. Describe the feel of your breathing—and whatever images come along with that feel (sight, sound, etc.), actual or imagined.

Can you feel your heartbeat or your pulse? Describe what either (or both) feels like, and any images or memories that come with that feeling.

A MIRROR: Imagine a mirror. Describe exactly what you see in your mind's eye–in the mirror, of the mirror, around the mirror. *Don't* describe (or explain) someone's *inner* self; you can't see that! What do you see, hear, etc.? Describe that. Keep it as a rule for description: describe what comes to your senses; that's all you *can* describe; the rest is explanation.

A ROOM: Imagine a room. Place someone in it. Describe room and person and how they are situated. (This is the essential situation of theater.)
- A door opens on the right.
- A door opens on the left.

18

A HOME: Imagine a home or home-like place. Put yourself in it. Explore this place, describing whatever rooms you enter, and whatever encounters you might have. (This can be an actual or imagined home.)

A DWELLING PLACE (constructed or natural): Imagine a place where you might stay, dwell for some time. Describe the setting and your place in it.

A CHILD: Imagine a child, give it a name. Describe. Put the child in some specific place. If you care to, bring someone into that place.

A YOUTH: Imagine a youth:
- walking down a hallway toward a door unnoticed until now
- or walking into the attic, or the basement
- searching through the house
- sitting down to a meal with the family
- walking toward a fast food restaurant.

GROUP RELATIONSHIP: List the groups you belong to. (The group should involve more than two persons but should be less than "the human race.") Pick a group that matters most to you at present. Describe your most significant experience in connection with this group. What other group has the most dynamic relationship with this group? Describe the most significant interaction you can recall or imagine between members of each group, even if that involves only two persons.

AN OPPOSITE: Imagine someone the opposite of yourself. Describe them within a particular setting. If it makes the description more real, imagine them standing or sitting opposite yourself.

SPECIAL OBJECT: Recall an object (of any sort) special to you, past or present. Describe it in detail. Include its setting, what surrounds it, if that seems important.

A VEHICLE: Imagine a vehicle (of any sort), the first that comes vividly to mind. Describe the vehicle inside and out.
   Who is in it? Who is driving? If you care to, take a trip.

JOURNEY: Imagine someone, some place, who wants to go somewhere. (That someone may be, or may not be, you. Begin a story of their trip or journey, perhaps with a description of the place they are leaving.

ANIMALS: Describe one animal (or more) out of the categories that follow, whichever strikes your imagination, or any other living creature that comes to mind. In your description include their environment (and perhaps their movements).

An insect or bug	A dog	A cat
A large mammal	A reptile	A sea creature
A bird	A carnivore	A grazing animal

NATURAL ENVIRONMENTS: Imagine, or observe, one or more of the natural environments listed, whichever brings vivid images (actual or imagined). Describe it:

- Earth: a plain, valley, mountain, etc.
- Water: a pond, lake, ocean, stream, river, etc.
- Sky: blue, cloudy, with rain or snow, etc.
- Plant life: woods, forest, meadow, field, garden, etc.

THE HEAVENS: Imagine looking up into the heavens at night. Or some cloudless night, just go out and look. Describe.

ANYTHING THAT CAPTURES YOUR ATTENTION: Any time at all, when you find a scene, place, person, or object that captures your attention, especially one that stirs feeling—stop, if you can, and describe what has drawn your attention.

Or go to a place that interests you, and describe it.

FREEWRITING: Every now and then, especially if you feel at a loss for subjects, just put your pen to paper and write absolutely whatever comes to mind. Keep your pen moving, even if you have to write that "nothing is coming to mind"; that's something. Something else will follow.

Perhaps you have a subject in mind, but for some reason can't get started. Try freewriting with your subject in mind.

AN IDEAL DAY: Imagine an ideal day, one that you can imagine living, sometime within the next two to eight years. Wake yourself up and "walk" yourself through your day descriptively, concentrating your description on just the most important events, persons, places, and things. Use a sentence or a short paragraph to bridge the writing from important event to important event. Don't merely do a diary of the entire day.

Perhaps you recall a day *actually* lived that seemed ideal. Describe that day using the suggestions above.

Or imagine one ideal day in a desired career.

NOTE: With each of these descriptions/imaginations resist the temptation to speak generally concerning the experience, to talk about *all* the times, *everyone and everything*, what it's *usually* like, what *could or would* happen. (Have you read this before? You have. But it's easily forgotten.) As soon as you talk about "all" and "usually," you are beginning to *explain*, to talk *about*—not to describe.

Be there as if it were happening just that one particular time and place. (This, too, is old advice, but extremely important.) Writing has a unique ability to make an experience come alive—become real—just in the description of concrete particulars: **one time, one thing, one person at a time.**

These imaginations may come from anywhere; let them. They may seem bizarre; let them be. (Symbols seem bizarre sometimes.) They may be of actual persons and places. Fine. All that counts is that they have occurred to you, that you have for some reason remembered them, and that you make them real in the writing.

That they have occurred to you—that doesn't sound important. But think: the operation of your mind is far more intricate and complex than the most powerful computer yet imagined. *Your* mind. What occurs to you is the result of billions of very complex mental interactions that rise to your awareness, finally, in mental images. Respect what just occurs to you; respect what your mind offers.

The chapter that follows will give some suggestions as to how to capture experience concretely.

3 DESCRIPTION: CAPTURING MENTAL IMAGES

When well written, my descriptive writings have given an almost immediate sensory response. One of my favorite examples of this is when I described someone's hair as "hanging wildly like over ripened grapes." I cannot think of anything better to more accurately describe it. Also, I described the rain as having "sewn the autumn leaves into a cold quilt of color." Over the last few months I've felt compelled to write about small things like this, which have inspired me. It has proven to be an excellent exercise.

Coalhouse

A paper without a sense of experience is like a cake without an icing.
A paper without a sense of experience is like a chicken soup made without chicken stock.

Yu Kurokawa

. . . to make you hear, to make you feel—it is, before all, to make you <u>see</u>. That—and no more, and it is everything.

Joseph Conrad, novelist

Voice alone can capture a great deal of experience, the "sound" of experience. But voice alone won't capture the full sense of experience; the other senses, especially sight, need to come into play, as they do in our day-to-day lives. Sight is a powerful human sense; in ancient Greek, to see meant to know. We still use "see" for knowing.

Description is not always easy. It's far easier to generalize, opinionate, jump to conclusions. But that's not satisfying, these writers suggest. And it makes for confusing, even disjointed papers that don't go anywhere, and that don't develop a theme.

Generalizations restrict "voice," because they don't give "voice" anywhere to go. With a series of generalizations you've got something like a series of topics every sentence or two, each with a new voice.

What makes generalizations even worse is that they are often stuffed with worn out, wrong ideas. And if they're right–your generalization won't confirm that you are right—or wrong. Description is necessary for writing to secure its ideas.

The essence of description is to capture the sight, sound, smell, taste and feel of experience, all the senses by means of which your mind encounters the world.

It is hot, so very hot. Yet there is a soft, cool breeze coming off the ocean. Somehow it seems to smooth the hot, sticky feeling in the air. There is a quietness, so quiet that I can hear the rustling of the palm trees, and the cry of the cockatoos. I can smell the sweet fragrance of orchids flourishing nearby. An old woman strolls by with a basket of fruit on her head. A group of boys playing with a soccer ball pass by. And across the road a young girl hangs out her wash. The sun has turned into a bright, orange ball sending a blizzard of colors across the sky. I watch as it slowly sinks behind the rich, green mountains. Settling back into my rocking chair and turning to my husband I say, "So this is Africa."

Linda Yeboah

Linda begins with touch; hearing, smell, then sight follow. Nice progression. She first gets in touch with her new environment, gets the feel of it, goes on to catch its sound and smell, and finally takes a more complete look at its features. This isn't complicated; one thing after another presents itself to her. She describes each by means of a dominant quality or two. Then, with a short sentence of conversation, she puts the experience in place. We get the experience as experienced. But if she had started, "This is what my first trip to Africa was like. It was hot, so very hot"—we might not have been drawn so easily into the scene.
Explanation ahead of description weakens it, and can kill it.

In previous chapters you've seen descriptions that are complex and dramatic. That's not required; descriptions just have to pay attention. What follows is a woman's description of an evening with her dog. Observe how closely her description pays attention to the experience.

My dog hops up onto "his spot" on the couch. Propping himself up against the arm he turns and looks at me. He can't get comfortable. My books are in his way. I move the books and he settles in. Groaning contentedly he rests his head on his front legs. He looks at me and closes his eyes.

I move closer to him, resting my arm on his side and my head on his rear leg. I watch his eyes; he is resting. His nose is pressed against the couch; I hear little rhythmic puffs of air. His eyelids flicker and open occasionally to sounds in the distance, a car door shutting, the sound of cars driving past, or honking.

With my thoughts of "what a good boy he is," he groans and nuzzles his nose deeper into the couch. He knows!

Tamera L.

Even the mention of a few sounds and sights gives this situation sense. "Groaning contentedly," and the "little rhythmic puffs of air" put us right there. She doesn't say, "His eyelids flicker and open occasionally to several sounds." She details those sounds: ". . . in the distance; a car door shutting, the sound of cars driving past, or honking." That *detail* puts us there, as it always does in description.

Sight is the dominant human sense; much of the brain is taken up processing images of sight. A young woman's description of her little brother follows; he has taken up karate.

A poised silhouette, barely visible down the narrow stretch of dim corridor, stands motionless. I curiously venture down the hallway to catch a better glimpse of this mysterious figure. A sense of uncertainty creeps in and fills the atmosphere like a thick fog. Step by step I bring myself closer to the human before me. I see in front of me a midget assassin, somewhat comical at first, but menacing nevertheless. Innocent but trained eyes glare at me. A corner of his mouth curves upward in a devilish smirk. Short strands of silky hair, like the fur on an electrified cat, glisten in the light flashing all around. My focal point drifts down from his soft face to the crisp, white uniform draped over his small frame. A black belt dangles in the stillness. He positions himself, left arm extended from his chest, right fist inverted and tucked back at his side. Taking a deep breath and exhaling, he cries out in a helium-induced voice, "these hands are lethal weapons!"

Anonymous

Observe the sharply detailed view of the "midget assassin."

My focal point drifts down from his soft face to the crisp, white uniform draped over his small frame. A black belt dangles in the stillness. He positions himself, left arm extended from his chest, right fist inverted and tucked back at his side.

The image is specific, detailed, even to the specifics of position: "left arm extended from his chest, right fist inverted and tucked back at his side." That's not easy: to present complex positioning. But it gives us the picture, exactly.

Metaphors help the description along: "midget assassin," silky hair "like the fur on an electrified cat," and "helium-induced voice."

Following is a paragraph from a journal entry describing the writer's first experience of bungee jumping. Feeling and sight dominate.

I continue to ascend the stairs. My chest is growing heavy. Near the sixth flight my knees start to shake and I have to grip the railing to continue on. I look down–bad idea–and spot the little ant with the camera. That would be my boyfriend. All eyes, it seems, are on me and my ascension. I feel like turning around and going down. To safety. The ground. Peace of mind. But my pride– or is it my thirst for adventure–forces me on. I'm nearing the top. When I reach the top I look around. I am high. Real high. How high, I'm not sure, but I can see the whole golf course next door, the water park beyond that, and hotels next to that. I see hundreds of broccoli-like trees and matchbox cars. The blood is rushing in my ears. My breathing is labored. Very labored. I think this is what drowning feels like.

Gina Ratini

This *does* recreate the experience, in part because she gives us the feel of it: "chest growing heavy;" "blood is rushing to my ears;" "My breathing is labored . . . this is what drowning feels like." Short fragments indicate her nervousness at the top: "I feel like turning around and going down. To safety. The ground."

Images of sight convey the height to which she has climbed: "broccoli-like trees and matchbox cars." Metaphors, again. A good metaphor paints the picture with a stroke.

The following writing also uses a few apt metaphors.

Cousin Tom and me plot the plan out. He's eight, I'm ten. We got experience in this. We're at the grandparents and the plan is to get our mitts on grandpa's Metaxa. It sits on the scummy after dinner dining room table. Big, long bottle--some magic stuff in it, we bet. The fathers and uncles and the Greek himself sit around smoking, belching, and whipping down beer and Metaxa. Beer we've had—it's the Metaxa for us.

Tom pokes me in the gut just outside the doorway. "We can do it—watch me. I'll get it."

"You sure?"

"Yeah. C'mon. Act stupid."

We circle the table, mouths shut. Nobody pays attention because the Greek just called the President a bastard again and all hell's breaking loose. The table's a junk pile—glasses, bottles, butts ground out in icky leftovers. I catch Tom slipping up on the Greek's left, real quiet, when his father yells, "Goddamn it, then go back to Greece!" Fast Tom makes his move and–whap! Oh brother. The Greek's got his arm, yanks it back.

"You want Metaxa?" the Greek asks real slow. His gray Hitler mustache doesn't even move. Tom's like a fish, all mouth, no sound. Then the Greek's staring at me. "You. Come here." I jump like his dog, trot to stand by Tom. The Greek chews his stub of cheap cigar, and blows smoke in our eyes so they hurt. We feel queasy.

"You drink Metaxa, you drink it right, huh?" He reaches over, grabs two glasses from hell, puts a good shot in each. An aunt breezes in on the way to the

kitchen, sizes it all up and shrieks, "Daddy!" He waves her off like she's a mosquito. "Won't hurt." Hands us each a glass. "One swallow."

Great.

"Glass up, tip, in, swallow—Yeah!"

Done. I'm not choking . . . still breathing . . . no feeling in my mouth—suddenly, burning, pinching pain—hot air rams into my gut; I'm choking, wheezing, eyes burning, hot tears running.

The Greek howls with laughter, roars till tears come down his face, till he's choking on cigar smoke, till the whole damned table is laughing with him, pounding fists, hands, bottles, laughing and laughing; and I'm laughing right with them.

Tom's still got the glass of Metaxa in his hand. He's not laughing.

Eileen Flynn

We are brought sensuously into this piece in a variety of ways: by sight, sound (including speech), taste, touch, and "voice."

Metaphors are also used effectively.

Tom's like a fish, all mouth, no sound.
I jump like his dog, trot to stand by Tom.
He waves her off like she's a mosquito.

These metaphors compact lots of sense into a few words: Tom standing there, mouth wide open, not a sound coming out, very much like a fish caught and hanging on a line; the girl's dog-like obedience to the Greek's command; and the aunt waved off like a mosquito.

Speech is also used, giving us a sharp sense of the kids and the Greek. Speech, the prime means of human interaction, provides immediate access to the human world, "describes" it. We have already begun to know the kids and the Greek by the way they talk. If a description involves persons talking—quote them.

The kids' talk is ungrammatical, and should be; it's the story of a 10-year-old kid.

The entry that follows describes a birthing, and uses a variety of descriptive devices.

Slowly, laboriously, she shaves my enormous belly. The water on the razor is ice cold and I flinch with each stroke. I no longer feel anxious and excited—fear has set in. Finally, after what seems like hours of poking and prodding, I am ready. Finally, ready for my great adventure.

26

I am off, wheeling down the corridor to what I think is certain doom. There is a catch in my throat. I must sound hoarse. The fear is bottled up. What exactly will they do to me?

The room is so brightly lit that it seems there must be spotlights on me. Everything, everything is cold, frozen. A soccer team of doctors and nurses stands over me. And a curtain, a big blue curtain, is draped over my chest blocking my view. One of the team members asks me a question. I reiterate his question and add my own; "where is my husband?"

"Can you feel this?" Again he says this.

"Where is my husband?" We go on like this. He must think I am over medicated. I don't care what he does or says. My god-damned husband should be here.

I can feel the scissors, or is it a knife, cutting through my skin. There is no pain. Layer after layer of skin and thin tissue is cut through. I am wide awake. I am shaking, frightened. Neither my body nor mind can comprehend what is about to happen.

"You'll feel some pulling now." I brace myself, my body at high intensity now. Again I feel the movements of the doctors, moving this time inside me. Groping, grasping, finally an intense pull—my body straining under this pressure. At last, I can feel him, my son, sliding through this artificial opening. His head, shoulders, hands, body, legs, feet. His cry, delicate and low pitched. I cannot see him. The curtain . . . the nurses moving quickly. He is behind me now. My arms pinned to a board, my face attached to an oxygen mask. I cannot turn. I can only hear him, his soft, struggling cries.

S.

"The razor is ice cold and I flinch with each stroke." The accents catch her fear right off. "There's a catch in my throat." (Sounds like that, doesn't it). Then the "soccer team of doctors and nurses." (A strong metaphor.) And the standup-comic humor:

" . . . where is my husband?"
"Can you feel this?" Again he says this
"Where is my husband?" We go on like this.

Her description of the birthing itself is sensitive and subtle. She feels the doctor reaching in for her child,

Groping, grasping, finally an intense pull--my body straining under this pressure. At last, I can feel him, my son, sliding through this artificial opening. His head, shoulders, hands, body, legs, feet. His cry, delicate and low pitched.

A fragment presents the birth itself, just as her child emerges. Another fragment, his cry.

Observe how finely she captures the moments that follow.

The curtain . . . the nurses moving quickly. He is behind me now. My arms pinned to a board, my face attached to an oxygen mask. I cannot turn. I can only hear him, his soft, struggling cries.

First a fragment for actions hidden from her, not in her grasp. Then a statement; she knows where he is. Then a fragment for her inability to move. Then statements: She can't turn, but she can hear her new-born son.

The following writing describes a woman's visit to her doctor.

Patiently I wait in the dull yellow room for the doctor to return. A nurse with curly blonde hair and so much mascara on that it's rubbing off onto her eyelid comes and says, "he'll be in, just a few more minutes."

Damn, I'm getting sick of looking at the same four yellow walls, a shelf full of Lassie pictures with gold trimming on the frames, and diplomas with that fancy writing that reminds me of ocean waves. How long does it take to get results from an annual pap smear and pee test? I might as well get comfortable and go to sleep, seeing that no one is rushing in here. These damn chairs are not so pleasing to sit in when your ass is wide. They have no cushioned seat, so I'm sitting on hard plastic, the arms are too close together, and I can't sit straight.

Finally, the knock on the door that I've been waiting for, almost like waiting for a check in the mail. I think, yes, tell me that I'm okay, make my next appointment in six months and–see ya! I'm out of here.

The door opens swiftly, and there is the blue-eyed, grey-haired man, very nicely tanned that is gonna save the day. Just hurry it up and I'll be on my merry way. He takes his gold and black trimmed glasses, puts them on and sits in his high back cushioned chair and looks at me with a nice little grin. He shuffles his folder full of papers, lets out a big sigh and says, "well the reason that you're having stomach aches and feeling funny is because you're one month pregnant."

Pregnant! Who's pregnant? Me? Can't be. He must have mixed up the results with someone else's.

"How do you feel about that? Okay?" he says. "I thought you were on birth control?"

"I thought I was, too," I say.

I was careful, but not enough, I guess. What am I gonna do? How can I take care of a child? I feel like someone just took all my hopes and dreams and shit on them.

28

Pregnant means my body will grow for nine months and I'll look like a hippopotamus. I'll be unshapely, fat and moody; or I might have a nice pregnancy and no complaints from me at all.

"Hello there," a voice says. "Are you okay?"

"I'm fine," I say.

"The nurse will make an appointment for you next month and give you prenatal tablets," he explains.

"Next month, why am I coming to you next month?" I ask.

"Oh, you have to come until you're six months, then weekly when you're close to your due date."

Due date? You mean these people already know when I'm going to have the baby? "When might that be? I ask.

"Oh, January," he says.

I'll be pregnant for my birthday, Christmas, and New Years. No more parties, no more drinking, no more nothing. I feel like I was just told I had to spend nine months in a nun's home.

"See you next month, MOM," the doctor says as he lets me out of the room.

"Yeah," I say with a little grin.

I'm walking out to the parking lot wondering how the hell am I gonna do this. I am pregnant and my whole life is about to change. I will not be able to "get up and go" anymore. Long trips are out of the question; staying the night at a friend's house will be no more.

So I cry, cry, like I just lost a best friend. I cry so much that I could've made a rainstorm. I just wanted my mommy. Mommies make everything better. I'm thinking that this person growing inside of me is going to call me mommy and depend on me for everything. Will I be able to handle it?

U. Thomas

Once she was done with her piece, Ms. Thomas was not at all sure that she had "gotten it," written a good descriptive piece. She got it, the sensuous particulars of her experience, the setting, her emotions, her thoughts in the moment, conversation, the character of the doctor (a classic), and her own character with a great sense of humor, quite evident in her voice.

Short Forms: Dramatic Monologues,
Dialogues, Sketches, Narratives and Reflections

Perhaps many of your journal writings (so far) seem formless, thoughts thrown together, a description, a memory, complaints, fragments of this and that. But forms of various sorts are always embedded in journal writing and emerging naturally through it.

Perhaps an awareness of just a few common forms will sharpen your sense of form, how a given experience finds its way to completion. Studying these forms, you may see ways to draw out the forms emerging in some of your more interesting journal writings, and make them more complete.

The exact labeling of these forms isn't important (or possible); dozens of terms could be used. Often, terms will cross boundaries, one form including or mixing with another. Story can be told by means of nearly all the forms listed in the section head above. One form may precipitate or evolve into another. But terms can at least give some idea of how certain forms handle experience.

Another reason to discuss and example short, informal writings such as these is to point up the crucial part that "voice" and description play in all forms.

Form pleases us, gives the writing a pleasing, finished shape.

The following piece is a **dramatic monologue.** Though others talk they don't talk for themselves (for the most part); the author, Jen, repeats or suggests what they say. Toward the end she allows a little **dialogue.** But with the monologue, the talk, and the bar, are entirely hers.

"Hi guys! What can I do you for? Of course I can pour a Guinness." I reach down to grab a pint glass. I love the feel of these things in the hand. The way my fingers fit around the base. And the weight is just perfect. I start the pour. Fill it only 1/3 up. "And what can I get for you? No Honey, I'm not married. Why do you ask?" I throw a kiss to an incoming regular. "No Baby, that kiss was not for you. Yes I have a boyfriend." I turn to pull on the long black tap. One inch from the top. "What did you want? A snakebite? What a coincidence, that's what my man drinks. No, you cannot take his place for the night!" A couple I know strolls to the other end of the bar. I run my eyes along the multitude of glasses to measure how much liquid is left in each. I see Tommy coming up the walkway outside. I pour him a porter. Place it on a napkin at the corner seat of the bar—his seat. "Hey Tom!" He throws me a smile when he sees his beer is ready and waiting, as usual. He looks tired. A salesman enters. "Hey you! Nice tie! Can I have it?" An arm waves from way over in the lounge. "I don't care where you bought it. I don't have thirty bucks to spend on a tie. I want the one around your neck!" I run to the kitchen for the group-of-five's appetizers. Up the stairs. Down the stairs. I

place the plates on the table. "Of course I can get you extra napkins. Does anyone need a refill? A porter and a Guinness, gotcha." I sprint to that tap, once again (I love this stuff!), finish off the afore mentioned gent's drink and start the next one. "You want shots? Hold on boys, I'm comin.'" Some broad croons, "Peel me a grape..." over the staticky speakers. "Hi girls! Be right witcha." (I'm amazing!) I deliver the pints to the party-of-five and check to see if they're happy with their food. I turn and bang smack-dab into some guy. "Hey! What about me?" This mother . . . does this every time. He just walked in the damn door! But I won't bitch, he's a good tipper. "What'll it be tonight? Same as last week?" He doesn't remember what he drank, but I do. I pour the single malt into a snifter with a side of water and place it in front of him. "WhatamI doin' later? Sorry. I have plans." I bolt to the other end of the bar. "Toldya I wouldn't forget ya. What'llya have, Ladies? Sorry we're out of strawberries. But I can make you a raspberry daiquiri. Three of 'em? Sure." I rush to the blender. Frozen drinks are such a pain in the ass! The appliance is too small, of course. I can only make two drinks at a time. Oh well. I empty ash trays, wiping them with a cocktail napkin. I see a woman reaching for her pack. Grabbing my lighter from my pocket as I walk, I step toward her and light her cigarette, just as she places it to her lips. She flinches then smiles and makes eye contact. Her fingers touch my hand ever so softly as she inhales deeply on the flame. I return to the blender. "Yes I smoke. No, you can't bum one. I can sell you a pack for three bucks? Look, Honey, I've got my looks. I'm working for money now." Laughter fills the room. Funny how people who are drinking will just follow suit. I deliver three whipped cream and cherry topped masterpieces to the Barbie dolls. "There you go. Love your hair." I clear dirty dishes from tables as I zoom by. Take refill orders. Empty more ashtrays. Carly Simon now. I sing along as I light more cigarettes. "I have a great voice? Thank you." I finish the song. "Tonto!" A very young, very cute pseudo-regular walks in with his buddies. He high-five's me. I pour their beer and deliver it. They are still standing. As I place the glasses on the table I am surrounded by six-foot, twenty-three-year-old athletic bodies. "God I love this job!" They laugh. My boss walks through the lounge, smiling. Everyone smiles back. She knows what an asset I am. A barely legal boy swaggers up to the bar. I recognize him. He is quite drunk. "Cam I hab a cap'm am coke, pleez Jem?" "Are you driving, Baby?" "I'm mot. Mai carr iz." "Wrong answer!" I turn to another customer. The drunk kid is chuckling. Good, I'm not in the mood for confrontation. "How's your daughter, Tom?" He beams. We chat. I clean more ashtrays, humming to myself. A group of four businessmen enter the room. Nice suits, expensive silk ties. "Cha-ching!" I clear a space for them at the bar. Light yet another cigarette. "Nice ass!" "My mother, my boyfriend and I thank you." "Nice tits! Are they real?" I guess money can't buy everything. I look at the clock. Over two hours to go . . .

Jen Johnston

Here are Jen's comments on her writing.

I call this paper "Epitome." It covers about one hour of me in a tie and really good shoes while performing at my last job. The idea came to me while sipping Dewars on my deck . . . I was reminiscing. I really do enjoy many aspects of tending bar. Obviously, there are many more I do not miss!

All of the quoted material is exact. I hope the fact that not one part of my body was still while any of this was taking place is evident.

I decided to keep the writing to a single paragraph because the experience as I wrote it seemed continuous, without a stop.

The dramatic monologue works well for the experience she is dealing with. It's her bar. With a dramatic monologue you've got complete control, even (as here) of someone else's talk. You filter, you represent, you make it yours. You also have the freedom to imagine what others are thinking as you talk. Dramatic monologue works well to present a scene such as this, all from one perspective, where thoughts, talk, and action tumble one upon the other without interruption. Toward the end the drunk kid and the businessmen respond to Jen's talk; creating dialogue. The quality of drunken speech needs to come through. And the business men are quite intrusive; they have disrupted the running monologue, and must be heard (unfortunately) in their own right. Dialogue intrudes; it's not entirely her bar anymore.

The writing that follows is a **sketch** of a dynamic relationship conveyed largely through the writer's dramatic voice. Sketches, in contrast to monologues and dialogues (and other narrative forms) attempt to cover more ground, to present a character or situation, even a life, but in a few strokes, in outline, with a few particulars that say it all. Specifics are important (as they always are with description/narration), but the specifics need to be significant, catching some essence of the person or situation. A sketch is a good form to consider if you want to get the picture in outline, like an artistic sketch, with color and detail missing.

Bobby

I've been thinking today about what I've written in my journal so far. I've decided that it's time to write something about the most important person in my life, my husband.

Bob and I met when I was fourteen and he was seventeen. From the very beginning we knew we were in love. There was never any question about whether or not we'd marry. We did it as soon as I turned eighteen. Wasn't nobody gonna talk us out of it.

32

In a way, we've grown up together. Bob's gone through some of the toughest times I've had with my family. In a world of complete @*%@* madness he was the safest place I'd ever found. That was thirty years ago. The things we've done to, for, and with each other since, are endless.

This man has cut my heart out, broken it, healed it, and filled it with love. He has the ability to make me happy beyond belief, or hurt me more than anyone else I've ever known.

We've clung to each other for support, and then pushed each other away when we needed someone the most.

I've stood in his face, head spinning, spitting fire, and said, "If I didn't know I'd go to jail, I'd cut your guts out and watch you bleed to death!" I've shadow boxed within a hair's width of his nose, when I was so pissed I knew if I ever hit him he'd never get up. But there's never been a time that I wouldn't defend or protect him against anything, or anybody.

He's made me love him when I didn't want to; he's made me hate him when I didn't want to.

He can say the wrong thing at the wrong time, the wrong thing at the right time, and the right thing at the wrong time. But worse than any of these is when he says nothing at all.

He knows things about me that nobody else knows, has seen things that nobody else has. He sees beyond my best, and has definitely lived through my absolute worst.

This man has let me down too many times to count, but when my father lay dying in our home, I could never have made it through without him. He made Daddy's death easier for him, and literally saved my life.

He's become someone I can't live without, but more important, he's someone I DON'T WANT to live without.

He promised me when we got married that he'd never go bald like his father, but he did. He promised me I'd never have to drive truck for our mail business; I drove for ten years. I love to talk; it takes an act of God to get him into a conversation. I hate reruns, he loves 'em. I hate to miss the news; it puts him to sleep. I love to read; it puts him to sleep. I hear everything; you gotta tell him everything at least twice. All in all I'd say we're just right for each other.

If anyone were to ask me how you make a marriage work, I'd have to say, "How the hell should I know?!" This ain't no science. Sometimes you can't tell the good guy from the bad guy, right from wrong, black from white. In fact the grey areas dominate.

Bob and I have stumbled, bumbled, climbed, and even reached the top. Everything in life will affect your journey. Nobody's will be just like ours. There's one thing I say, though; the view at the top is worth the trip.

When people have said to us that we don't understand what having real problems are like, we just smile at each other, and REMEMBER.

Dianna

33

When I wrote this paper about my husband, I had nothing particular in mind to write. When I was finished and I read it through, I saw it was full of contrasts.

I'm not sure if it's "descriptive." Going over all my papers, though, I find myself describing feelings and emotions constantly. No matter what situation I find myself in, in life, I see and remember feelings. Mine or anybody that is involved. Everything else seems like so much window dressing.

When I was writing, I wanted to conjure lots of feelings, and maybe a picture or two. I tried to describe what I think marriage is, a lesson in contrasts.

First a comment on the form that she mentions, contrasts. It's full of them. But this makes perfect sense; her marriage (marriage itself, she says) is full of contrasts. The structure of her sentences heightens these contrasts.

This man has cut my heart out, broken it, healed it, and filled it with love. He has the ability to make me happy beyond belief, or hurt me more than anyone else I've ever known.

He's made me love him when I didn't want to; he's made me hate him when I didn't want to.

He promised me when we got married that he'd never go bald like his father, but he did. He promised me I'd never have to drive truck for our mail business; I drove for ten years. I love to talk; it takes an act of God to get him into a conversation.

These contrasts are presented with great humor, partly conveyed through exaggeration. Descriptive detail counts here as well. Just six paragraphs into her piece she gives us a vivid, brief picture of their interaction.

I've stood in his face, head spinning, spitting fire, and said, "If I didn't know I'd go to jail, I'd cut your guts out and watch you bleed to death!" I've shadow boxed within a hair's width of his nose, when I was so pissed I knew if I ever hit him he'd never get up.

"Voice" plays a huge part in this sketch, characterizing the relationship, and Dianna as author: bright, gutsy, humorous, and playful. Her "voice" is descriptive (as voice is), giving us a sharp sense of the tone, rhythm, pace, pitch, and intensity, of a marriage.

The next piece is a **sketch** of a young Korean woman's relationship with her brother as he grows into adolescence.

When I went back home last winter, I found my brother had unfortunately become a typical teenager. I had been expecting my lovely little bro to dart

34

right out of the house like a puppy and give me a big, sticky hug. Instead, a boy with a baby face that didn't really suit his long, thin limbs was there. He stayed out of two-meter radius from me and grunted when I asked him to help me carry my trunk. "Welcome back, sis." That was all he said.

My brother used to be the sweetest creature on the earth. Right from the moment he was born, he already had bushels of shiny black hair. When he shed his red, wrinkled new-born baby skin, his face revealed incredibly long eye lashes, skin as soft and white as porcelain, cherry lips, and smile that turned his big eyes into lovely crescents. The guests didn't make the polite, obligatory comment "Your daughter is cute," but showed genuine surprise. "Why, your son's a beaut!" Cashiers at the mall begged Mom to let them hold him for a second, and once a person from an advertising company spotted him and asked Mom if she'd be interested to register him for audition in a modeling agency. By the time he was in the kindergarten, day-by-day next-door girls rang our doorbell and shyly asked whether Heeseob was home. Of course, from time to time, I was jealous. Thrown down from my throne as the only child, I could have taken revenge by using common bad sister tactics such as pinching him really hard when Grandma looked away or screaming when he colored my homework with Mom's lipstick. But he was too sweet. Way too sweet. He ran after me, wanted to do whatever I was doing, and when I got back from school, he threw himself into my arms breathlessly, his cheeks red with excitement.

But now, my 11-year-old brother was sulky, had hairy legs and a voice undergoing transformation from mezzo-soprano to tenor. "Well, he has been an angel so far," Mom sighed, as he locked himself in his room. "And now it's time for us to pay."

Thus during my six-month stay at home, I witnessed how a seraphic boy without wings turned into a teenager with a devilish temper. I also felt so sorry for Mom, for I had gone through a similar transformation during my middle school and high school years. The only difference was that I yelled more. My bro sulked more. "Whatever" and "So what?" had become his answer to everything.

But everyday, when he came home from school, he had tons of 'amazing' stories to tell me, just like he had been a year ago. He excitedly talked about how one of his classmates fought an 8th-grader and won; how he got a good grade in a science test but a dismal score in a math test; how he came in second (out of four total participants) in a 100-m race; and how he played computer games with his computer game-savvy friend and almost beat him. During these conversations, I was almost convinced he was back to his normal self. But when he had no more to tell me, or when I gave him a "stupid" response, my dear brother growled, put on his grimace, and locked himself in his room until he got hungry.

Once I caught him eagerly examining his face in the mirror. Turned out there was a pimple on his forehead. I told him to wash his face more often and

35

he immediately hit back, saying I was the one covered with erupting volcanoes of pimples. In that very evening he smothered his face with my anti-acne foam cleanser. While he was eagerly rubbing his cheeks with foam, he had found me grinning behind him and gave me his usual response—slamming the door shut. Nonetheless, he kept using my anti-acne cleanser every night.   Pimples eventually disappeared, but soon right above his upper lip grew the unmistakable, darkening presence of a future moustache, which he eyed with great pleasure.

On the morning I departed Korea for Mount Holyoke, I found him slumped on his bed, snoring. It was five in the morning. I woke him up, said good-bye, gave him a hug and a gift, and was ready for an equally decent farewell. But he merely yawned, muttered, "OK, see ya," and then fell back on his bed. For a moment, I seriously considered giving him a kick. As I was lifting my foot to deliver a good one, I noticed his back and shoulder were much broader than I thought. Only one year ago, my brother, then a little boy, had followed me all the way to the airport and even the port exit. When Dad told him it's time to say goodbye, he stood there without saying anything, biting his lips. His small, pale face has been imprinted in my memory since then. Gee, I thought, coming back to reality, he did grow up, didn't he.

Last Friday I called him. "Hi," said my brooding teenage brother. In the background was the deafening noise of some cinematic catastrophe. I could easily imagine him watching TV, probably with his eyes fixed on the screen while holding up the phone. Bad timing. My fault. But the conversation had to be carried out, so I awkwardly asked him how he was.

Apparently he was very happy to have my cell phone. And wasn't very happy that I'd be able to see the fourth Harry Potter movie before him. "Have you done your homework?" I asked. He just gave me a familiar grunt. Then I hesitated and made a daring attempt, "I miss you very much." There was a brief silence on the other side of the phone. "You will be back in December anyways. Right?" Although it came with the jingles of TV commercial and the usual nonchalance of a teenager, his voice sounded kind of cracked.

Eunji

Again, observe that "voice" plays a big part in characterizing the author's attitude towards her brother, a loving, understanding voice at first, and later an ironic voice laced with humor:

But now, my 11-year-old brother was sulky, had hairy legs and a voice undergoing transformation from mezzo-soprano to tenor. "Well, he has been an angel so far," Mom sighed, as he locked up himself in his room. "And now it's time for us to pay."

36

Description also plays an important part in this piece, characterizing the change in her brother.

When he shed his red, wrinkled new-born baby skin, his face revealed incredibly long eye lashes, skin as soft and white as porcelain, cherry lips, and smile that turned his big eyes into lovely crescents.

A sketch seems the right form for these subjects. Neither writer goes into detailed description of the incidents they refer to, or into an extended description of just one incident. They give a picture in a few strokes (a sketch) of an entire relationship.

Narrative, a story of any sort, is one of the most common forms that journal writing might take, and one of the oldest forms within which we have captured our awareness of human life. **Dialogue** is often used, descriptive as it is of character. Narrative can range from reports of actual events to fiction. A good narrative will give us concrete particulars, the moments that make the events real.

The following narrative comes out of an actual situation, but the particular situation described (though realistic) is *fictional*. The author "tried to imagine the range of emotions that the family went through," and added "some of [his] own ideas or feelings as to what it's like to deal with that situation on an everyday basis."

Here I am again. Well, the here is not exactly the same but the situation is, again. I'm face to face with a cop who, from the looks of his shirt, would rather be face to face with his half eaten donut than me. I'm getting the usual rhetoric in monotone about how I should handle my "older" brother's little problems. Wow...that's how shitty he looks; people assume I'm his "little" brother. I've got him by six years but he's done such a job on himself, he looks old and used and gray.

The over nourished cop's telling me about the programs and the rehabs that he should get into soon. I want to say to him, "Look, shove it, okay; every program he's ever entered, he's either left, bluffed through or just served up stories so incredulous about the happenings inside that I was beginning to wonder if they were fueling his habit." But as usual, I'm calm and courteous and keep my mouth shut. Not smart to spurn possible help, right?

I'm informed that they're almost through processing him and he'll be mine shortly...swell. So I take my usual place on a bench in the waiting area. The person next to me is always different but the distraught expression is the same. I know what comes next but can't help wondering why these things can't take place during a "decent" hour. The "game" will be starting soon. Explanation galore for the unexplainable and I'll play my role to perfection.

I start to wonder about all the times I've been through this with my "older" brother and I'm staggered by the number. I actually plan for these fun-filled affairs in my monthly budget. I try amusing myself for the next twenty minutes or so by perusing the elegant collection of pictures and poetry done by the other misunderstood people held here. I'd hate to think that I missed out on a good poem about bowel movements and their resemblance to certain law enforcement officials.

Finally, a door opens and there he is in his wet, crusted, glowing splendor with his usual damned smirk and probing yellow eyes. Is it a sad thing that the sight of him no longer shocks me? He starts to speak but I sharply throw up a hand and mutter, "not here, not now." He follows me out to the Jeep and we partake in our usual custom: rolling the windows down and breaking out the trash bag. It's January.

I feel him watching me, looking for an opening to start his newest tale of woe. He's ready to speak. I can tell because he stopped moving his legs up and down and transferred that energy to his mouth. I shoot him a look and say, "No." This buys a few more minutes of silence but I haven't been able to shake this tremendous anger and for the first time am rapidly losing control of it. It doesn't hold, he starts to speak and I see red and hear the snap in the back of my head.

I lay into him fast. "Don't say a god damned thing or I swear to Christ, I'll pull over and kick the shit out of you. Again, we have to do this: police, lawyers, court, money bullshit. I'm so completely fed up with you, you useless, wasted jerkoff. God, Joey, Mom and Dad want nothing to do with you after every shitty thing imaginable was done to them by their own son. Don't you have any shame or respect for us or you?" He goes to speak, but I stop him again, "don't you say a god damned thing, don't you give me a reason to stop this car and kick your ass. You make me sick. I'm so tired of bailing your drunken ass out of jail. If you're not getting high or drunk, you're beating the shit out of some girl who's stupid enough to think she can help you, or you take your drug-induced rage out on animals because everyone else but me has given up on you and left. Christ, why can't you get it together?"

He seems stunned into silence but I'm not foolish enough to think that'll last. I'm foolish about a lot of things with him but I know he can't keep his mouth shut so I keep going. "Rehab after rehab, meeting after meeting . . . big deal. So you've admitted being a drug addict and a drunk to a roomful of strangers; so this justifies you being a lecherous and abusive waste of space. No more of this. God, all the money you stole from Sara and the damage you caused that you never helped pay for let alone help clean up. You've used everyone who's ever loved you. It's over. Everything you've owned and all the money you've ever had has been sent up your nasal cavity or floated inside a bottle. How do you do it? You're a loser, Joey. I never thought I'd say it but you're worse than a loser. Most losers have families; after tonight, you don't. Look at you, you threw up all over yourself; I smell the distinct odor of urine and even that mess can't hide the fact that you're skin is gray. How can you stand yourself? You're pathetic and I'm not wasting time on you.

You are helpless, weak-willed, useless, abusive and now out of luck. I was the last person on the planet who'd ever go to bat for you. It's over, Joey. It's over, no more."

Joey speaks and I go ahead and let him, "Hey, come on, we're brothers. You're going to let this little problem ruin our relationship?"

Wow, here's a surprise, an addict using guilt to get what he needs. I'm thinking of responding but decide to let it hang there. He doesn't get it, probably never will. I just stop talking and the ride to wherever I'm dropping him slips by in silence. I start to think about how he was when we were growing up and how he is now. He's not the same person, he never will be. The drugs and booze ate that guy away. I can't ever remember feeling this conflicted in my life. He is right. He's my brother and I love him. It kills me to do this but what am I suppose to do now that I haven't done?

He tells me to pull over and as he gets out, I hand him my coat. He stoops over and looks into the Jeep one more time, turns, and walks away. I want to yell, "Please, please get help before you die," but I keep it to myself because it won't matter. I drive home slowly. It's tough to see the road through tears.

Scott Peterson

About writing this piece, Scott says, "I tried to imagine walking and talking myself through a situation like this and what feelings would arise. It was tougher than I thought." This narrative does what a good narrative should do: it brings us into the (imagined) experience as if we were there, gives us the moments of the experience so that its flavor is unmistakable. Scott does this through devices that should be quite familiar by now: "voice," unmistakably showing Scott's disgust with the situation; dialogue (short as it is) that captures the conversation with his brother; and descriptions that give us the moments, both of his thinking and of the events.

The *particular* scene Scott describes is fictional, but it is a composite of many actual events like it, making the piece realistic.

The piece that follows could be called a **reflection,** since it concentrates thought on its subject, calmly, offering observations one by one. It's a story as well, a "once upon a time" story with its use of repetition and spare description.

In the Little Green House Down the Street

In the little green house down the street lives a family, a mother, father, and two children, a girl and a boy. I know of the family, but don't know much about them. I see the mother around with the kids; and the father, well I really don't know very much about him except what he looks like. I see them in church from time to time.

The little green house down the street is not very big and doesn't really stand out. There is a large birch tree that sits on the front lawn with a swing hanging from one of the branches, and a colorful flower bed that lines the driveway. In the driveway sits a van that the mother takes her children to school in every day. To the side of the house is a narrow walkway lined with shrubs that leads to the kitchen door the family uses to enter the house. I've never been inside but assume it's warm and cozy.

The little green house down the street, I pass by it many times a day never really taking notice. But after I heard the news, the news that the woman has cancer, now when I pass the house my eyes are drawn to it. I don't know why. I don't know what to expect to see; I just look. Now when I pass I say a prayer that her family will have the strength to endure the sadness that will soon be upon them.

In the little green house down the street lives a woman who knows soon she'll meet her maker. She was told recently that she has cancer, the kind that grows fast, and she doesn't have long to live. There's a mother who must come to terms with the fact she will leave behind her most prized possessions. She won't be there to help them grow up. She won't help pick out a prom dress, or go to baseball games. She won't see them graduate from high school and college. She won't see them walk down the aisle, or hold her first grandchild.

In the little green house down the street live two little children still too young to understand what forever is. They play in the yard; they look so carefree, swinging and running about. But I often wonder just how carefree they really are; do they realize that this will be the last spring they will spend with their mom? They have to take the school bus each morning now, because their mom is too sick to drive.

In the little green house down the street lives a man who has to go off to work each day as if nothing has changed. He has to keep working; cancer treatments aren't cheap you know. He has to watch other people, friends and family, take his wife for treatments, even though he wishes he could be the one to do it. There's a man who will soon also become a mom.

By the little green house down the street, I noticed one day a woman with white hair. She is the mother of the woman who lives there. I saw her helping her daughter out of the car after one of her treatments. I can just imagine, being a mom myself, what she was thinking: this is all backwards; I should be the sick one, not my daughter. Children shouldn't die before their parents. Why doesn't God take me instead? She has so much more to do in life. She takes her daughter's arm and helps her walk inside.

In the little green house down the street lives a woman who I am told is incredible. People say she never thinks about herself. They say she keeps fighting and her spirits are high. They say she never asks, "Why me?" She just keeps going.

The little green house down the street, I passed it today. There were many cars parked outside. I noticed that one of them stood out from the rest; it was long and black. And just as I was passing I saw the man, his two children, and the woman

40

with the white hair, getting out of it. I watched as they walked up the narrow path that leads to the kitchen of the warm cozy house that will never be the same.
In the little green house down the street lives a man and his two children.

E. McCann

About this reflection Ms. McCann wrote: *My idea for this story came from, well, different parts of me. Some of it came from things I experienced in my own life. I was thinking that we pass by houses of people that live close to us, and we don't know the people or what is happening inside the house.*

I wanted to create something that everyone would be able to understand and be touched by. I first wanted to write a poem, but haven't quite mastered the technique. So I thought, a short story telling how this kind of situation would affect not only the sick person but everyone around them as well.

I had to put myself in as the narrator, and tell how I felt each of these people would feel. When it came to the mother I used my own mother as a guide. Several years ago I lost a brother to cancer and remembered how my mother reacted to it. I thought about my own kids and how they would feel, and also my husband.

This writing was very emotional for me because I have been through it with my own family; I had a hard time getting through it. When it came to the repetitive phrase, "The little green house," I can't tell you why I used it; it just seemed right.

The voice in this piece is quiet and reflective, with no dramatics, just spare descriptions and observations simply put, presenting only the essentials.

The little green house down the street is not very big and doesn't really stand out. There is a large birch tree that sits on the front lawn with a swing hanging from one of the branches, and a colorful flowerbed . . .

The setting could be your neighborhood, anyone's, which gives the piece a homey, "you know this neighborhood," tone. The repetition of, "The little green house down the street," intensifies the implication: this is just one of the humble houses in the neighborhood, anyone's neighborhood.

The progression is also quiet, simple, and telling in its universality: a woman, two little children, a man, a mother, then the black car parked outside, and finally, "a man and his two children."

The Detail Dragon

For over a month, a student in one of my classes resisted the idea that descriptive details were important to writing, no matter how hard I tried to drive the idea home. Then one day Peter handed me this story.

Once upon a time there was a big, big, ugly dragon named Scott. He had long, pointy teeth and huge flaring nostrils at the end of his stubby, ridged snout. Great, gaping sockets where his eyes should have been, and shriveled folds of flesh, the leathery remnants of what were once ears. His body was a disarranged mass of gristle and bone shielded beneath countless corroded scales.

Scott was a hungry dragon. Not hungry in the ordinary sense, though. You see, Scott was a heartless, editor dragon. What Scott hungered for was (of course) details. And when he found them (slurp) he swallowed them up.

He tore across the land terrifying villagers, and roaring "Details! Details! Give me concrete imagery. Be sensuous!"

"God, what a bore; you've lost my interest completely," he would say when he found no details.

Wherever there were details, there was Scott to gobble them. A vast field with myriads of wild flowers. Huge red ones. Slurp. Lush multi-petaled yellow ones. Slurp. Teeny, tiny pink and purple ones with tiny, white, puff centers. Schleerp . . . brup! When he was done all that was left was a field. Just an ordinary, you know, field.

Now in this kingdom there was a princess and she was—well, you know, a princess. Nice figure, pretty hair, lots of nice things like that. Kind of boring, huh? Well, you see, that was the problem. With the dragon tromping all over the kingdom, gobbling all the details, the princess was—boring, and bored silly.

So one day she wrote a message to be sent to all corners of the kingdom. It read "HELP," and was signed, "The Princess."

Now as it happened there was a knight in this kingdom. When he saw the message he decided to go see what it was about. So he grabbed his sword and rode off to the princess's castle.

When he arrived she said, "Hello."

And he said, "I saw your message."

And she said, "It's that horrible, nasty, awful dragon; he's gobbled all my wonderful details." And then she burst into tears. Great sobs racked her body, tears streamed down her face.

Instantly Scott appeared, huge, tattered wings beating the air, half-eaten chunks of detail dribbling from the corners of his ravenous maw and plop-plopping onto the ground.

The knight bounded off his horse and with a mighty swing of his sword slashed the dragon's throat.

42

The dragon bled . . . and died. And as his dark, red blood splashed out over the flagstones of the courtyard, the kingdom began to regain detail. The tall, lantern-jawed knight wiped his shining sword on the bright, green grass and returned it to its battered, leather scabbard. The curvaceous, young princess brushed her wild black hair back out of her doe-brown eyes. The robins in the apple orchard puffed out their bright, orange chests and sang "tweet, tweet, tweeteeteet." The crickets chirped "skeet-click-click-skeet." The flowers bloomed: big red ones, bright, multi-petalled yellow ones, and even little, tiny purple and pink ones with little white puffs in their centers.

Of course, with the dragon dead things changed. The princess realized that it wasn't practical (or fashionable) to go on living in a drafty, old castle. So she sold the nasty, old thing and moved into a plush, five-room condo ten minutes from the club district.
Our brave, lantern-jawed knight gave up riding around town on a white horse and settled in as a reform politician, slaying dragons of an entirely different sort.
As for the rest of our little kingdom, they soon forgot about the dragon and settled back into their comfortable rut: eggs for breakfast, meat loaf for dinner. They trotted around the house in pink, fuzzy slippers and made eyes at the mailman. Or went off to work with their beer guts resting on the steering wheels of their four-year old Fords, too busy to remember such a small detail as the death of a dragon.

Peter

Details, concrete and sensuous, are the essence of existence. So, kill the detail-eating dragon and enrich your writing kingdom. Avoid the easily stated opinion, the casual judgment, the quick explanation. It's much too easy to generalize and think that you've made sense. With generalizations you haven't made *sense;* you've taken leave of your senses. William Blake, the poet, put in starkly: "To generalize is to be an idiot."

To generalize only is to lose "touch" with experience, to lose the sense of experience. Life—is *life*—in its sensuous particulars.

What are you drawn to with feeling? What do you find yourself drawn to and dwelling on as you go about your life? Stop: observe, listen; your mind is at work on some aspect of your experience.

Describe what captures your attention, what your mind presents, just as it presents itself to you through your senses: a scene, a person, a happening little or large, an imagination, a dream.

Reject the impulse to talk *about* your description right off, using opinions, judgments and conclusions. Reject the impulse to quickly explain, as if you knew immediately what was what. You may. But you may find yourself just rehashing old ideas, perhaps ideas that haven't (ever) worked. If you feel the need to explain, to talk about the whys, wherefores, causes or effects, keep it brief—and get back to your description.

Be there in just one experience at one time, alive to all of it. The present tense will make it more immediate, perhaps more real. But use past tense if that seems right. Present the experience, re-present it to yourself on paper. New thoughts will emerge, thoughts more closely in touch with experience.

This is old advice. But the habit of making easy explanations too easily maintains itself. Break it with attention to your senses. As you've seen so far, and will see in the next chapter, the satisfaction of sense is not small.

4 EXPLORING DESCRIPTIONS FOR MEANING

A critique? You want a critique? If I had to criticize anything in the text it would have to be the difficulty in grasping, at first, the concept of "drawing out meanings." I couldn't enter this idea into my brain, that the words we use, and how we use them, mean something. But in the end—after I'd written the image down and simply asked myself what I thought it all meant, being careful not to take it literally (using metaphors), and after many hours of writing and continually going back to the text—the light finally came on. Then the flow of other images further illustrating the "meaning" arrived in buckets full.

Angel P.

. . . pick out a theme in our journal. Well, I thought I had two of them, Jay and my grandmother. But as I wrote more into the paper, I found out that they weren't my main theme at all; they were just contributing factors to my theme. I found out that I had been subtly talking about my abuse as a child the whole time. I never realized it till after this paper.

Sarah L.

The unconscious wants truth, as the body does.   *Adrienne Rich, poet*

As I revised my paper, I realized what symbolism I had written. It amazes me to think of just how much meaning certain words have. I kept this in mind when I reread this paper . . . I learned that I need to be more aware of symbolism. Here I am writing and not really understanding the true meaning of what I've written.

T. H.

. . . what thinking means . . . it is just putting this and that together; it is just saying one thing in terms of another.

Robert Frost

The free interplay of concepts and sense impressions.   *Albert Einstein on thinking*

Every object that emerges into the focus of our attention has meaning beyond the fact in which it figures.

Susanne Langer, Philosopher

"Here I am writing and not really understanding the true meaning of what I've written." This quote sets the agenda for this chapter: to explore what it means to make meaning from mental images.

The mind continually constructs *mental images* of its encounter with the world, images that present the drama of life at present (our fears, hopes and realities) and the impact of the past on the present. These images take all sorts of forms: objects, scenes and activities, memories, imaginations, and dreams. The purpose of images—in all of their forms—is the same: to see what is not actually visible, to touch the intangible, to make the unfamiliar familiar, the unknown known. That is, to make meaning of our uniquely human experience. That's intangible; but the mind makes it tangible with images.

Susanne Langer writes, "Every object that emerges into the focus of our attention has meaning" beyond its concrete existence. Every object or action or person to which we give attention has meaning beyond itself.

Valuing Images:
I'm going to spend a little time talking about the value of images because they are so easily dismissed. Shelly, the author of the piece below, is reviewing four months of writing, especially one of her descriptions. She happens to have written about a woman (an "object") who focused her attention:

> . . . *the old woman across the street who comes over to see the kids and fold my laundry. Factually that's true but now I realize all of the emotions in this paper were my own coming through. I state, "She's lonely. She just needs someone to listen to what she's thinking." I can still distinctly remember how full of emotion I was during the time that this paper was written, and it is clear that these emotions bubbled over in my writing, without me even realizing it at the time. (Isn't that amazing?!)*
> . . . *I can see that part of the old woman I wrote about was very symbolic of myself and my life. The writing starts, "It's freezing cold outside. The middle of winter. Grey. Dismal." Not only was this paper actually written in February, the middle of winter, but it was also a very cold, grey, and dismal period of my life due to being unhappy in my marriage. I referred to her as a "shadow of an old woman," feeling like a "shadow" myself during this time, not a complete, vibrant person.*
> "Alone again," I write describing the old woman. "This time he's not coming back." Again a very symbolic statement; my husband and I had disconnected and deep down inside I knew we wouldn't salvage our

46

relationship. "Loneliness is starting to drive her crazy. All she has is sitting and thinking and crying." All of these statements directly reflect me during that particular time in my life, even though I was writing a sketch of someone else's life.

Shelly

Objects we attend to, especially when they strike us with strong feeling, are symbolic, carrying personal meaning.

But our lives press in on us; we've got things to do this minute, hour, day. Are images worth stopping for long enough to write them down? And that journal—haven't we got a pretty good grasp on what's going on in our lives? A former student, now a poet, who knew the value of images and was expert in their interpretation, writes,

Recently I was involved in a relationship, which delighted but also troubled and confused me. It had been two years since I kept a journal and I saw no need to—I had, I thought, a keen understanding of my situation and my feelings toward it. I was wrong. Within weeks of beginning a new journal, six months of actions and reactions sorted themselves into sense.

I recorded a recurring, just-before-sleep image of a Christmas tree ornament (similar to one I'd seen as a child)—a little, crystal bird in a cage of twisted strands of glass. The cage was fragile, but the bird seemed sturdy. She sat on a golden perch connected by a chain of tiny gold links to the top of the cage. The door to the cage was open, in fact missing, allowing easy exit for the bird, whose wings were slightly raised, as if prepared to fly.

Cyndi Q.

Cyndi has captured a detailed sense of a crystal bird on a golden perch in a cage of glass—*un*like her life, actually, an image she might easily have dismissed as trivial. But she didn't. (Good thing.)

It didn't take me long to realize that the bird was me. My "cage" was my lovely, but fragile and "twisted" relationship. Although my "golden perch" was enjoyable and enviable, my position was "clearly" "ornamental" and strictly seasonal. The door, however, was open. The golden perch was chained, "linked" to the cage, but I was not. I was free to "fly" before I, like the glass bird, could be dropped or broken, or put away after the "holiday."

What came as a surprise to me was that the bird's wings were raised. The option my conscious mind had avoided—flight—was already acknowledged and prepared for by my subconscious.

Personal freedom is at stake here; the image suggests strongly what action she needs to take. You may be beyond devaluing your images, but the tendency to

47

dismiss them often lingers. I still find myself dismissing dreams, etc., that don't seem—on the surface—to mean much. That's a mistake, I find, most always.

Let's take a close reading of this image to see what it shows. Her mind is showing her three things: the *situation*, the possibility of (or tendency to) *action*, and the *qualities* of the situation and of the action. Let's take them one at a time.

Her **situation**: She is caged, her "perch" chained, but the door is open. This is how things "sit."

The possibility of (or tendency to) **action**: She can fly out if she wishes. This is what's happening, or could happen.

The **qualities** (of situation and action): Her cage is twisted but fragile. Her "perch," how she "sits" in the relationship, is "golden," rich. She is sturdy but strictly "ornamental," and "seasonal," a "holiday" bird (perhaps a "love bird"). This is what the situation and action are *like*.

Is there only *one* meaning to draw from a description, the "right" meaning? Cynthia is drawing out just *these* meanings with her cage. But she could have made others. She might have liked the cage, her golden perch, the holiday atmosphere—and decided that she wanted to stay right there, even if she might be "dropped" after the "holidays." More than one "right" meaning can be drawn from any image or description.

However, an image will usually *suggest* a meaning, sometimes clearly, though a feel and an eye are necessary for what the image seems to suggest. That may take some exploring, thinking back and forth between the image and your life until it fits a life situation or theme. Trust this: that the vital force moving you through life will drive toward meanings best for you, most truthful to experience. The mind is persistent, patient, and kind in this activity. It is concerned basically with our vitality, that we *live*, fully. To call upon an ancient scripture: the mind's concern is to know the truth of experience, and in that knowledge, find freedom.

Securing a meaning that you're happy with may involve being open to several images commenting on different aspects of the situation. (Much more on this in Chapter 5.) A married woman, Cynthia, describes in her journal the memory of an event/nonevent with her dentist husband, sparrows she noticed one afternoon outside her window, and a dream of a black box—these things that focused her attention enough to be written in the first pages of her journal.

Her dentist husband has pulled a few of her teeth, she writes, but hasn't done the bridgework to replace them, though she's asked, repeatedly. He's been saying–for two years–that he will, but hasn't. When she smiles, the gap shows, destroying her looks.

She thinks about this, and soon realizes that her teeth play a big part in her sense of identity, her beauty, and what she calls her "bite." Married life has taken part of her identity, her beauty and her "bite."

Next she writes a seemingly casual description. Sitting in her family room one afternoon, she describes just what she observes out the window, ordinary sparrows. But looking closely she sees more.

> . . . *cream and chocolate, beige and grey, black and white patterns like mosaics upon their feathers, each one different, each one lovely in its own distinct way. Subtle, but complex. Intricate and beautiful. A bird of paradise should be so lucky.*
>
> *And they have courage. When other birds turn and fly from a mere hint of winter, sparrows tough it out. They stay and face the weather, determined to make it to the spring.*

Before she's done with the description she knows that she's describing herself, a sense of her not-so-obvious beauty, and early inklings of her own courage in face of a potential divorce. She too may face a "winter," but like the sparrows, "tough it out." Later, in her journal, she records a dream.

> *I see a black box, like a geometric cube, about a foot square. As I open its hinged top a bunch of brightly colored balloons, the strings tied together, floats out of the box, up and away. For some reason this is so terrifying to me that I wake up in a cold sweat.*

Meaning is not immediately clear; but she works with it.

> *The black box seems to represent something square or solid in my life, but something I dislike, that I view in "black," perhaps something dark and sinister. The balloons are light and brightly colored. They <u>rise above</u> and <u>escape</u> the black box. They are like my emotions, my good feelings, that have been contained by my stable but "black" situation (most likely a comment on my marriage). I think what frightens me in this dream is not the balloons (the feelings) themselves, but more the loss of control over them, the fear that they are getting away from me.*

The record of a happening, a casual description, and a dream, all these have a common purpose: to begin to reveal the (invisible) situation between herself and her husband, giving her a picture of what's developing. These personal situations, the entire range of human interactions and perceptions of self, are difficult to "see." But that's just what the mind goes about doing with mental images.

Especially with the keeping of a journal the mind has time and place to work a theme. Cynthia has made a start; all sorts of writings in her journal continued to develop this theme. (Two of her dreams are recorded later this chapter.)

49

Before taking a close look at the process, consider what writing itself has to offer as a medium for making meaning. All the arts make meaning of human life in various ways. Dance, sculpture, music, painting, photography, film, drama, story, poetry, and personal essay, each gives us special images of what it means to be human. But with the verbal mediums of story, drama, poetry, and essay, meaning resides in words, the primary medium we humans use to communicate and to think. Writing concentrates language, focuses it sharply on the subject at hand. Writing serves meaning well.

The following writing began with distrust, the writer apparently having nothing meaningful to write. Armando's "method" is one way into the process.

I don't think I'm doing too well with this meaning thing. I don't know what is required, either. OK. An image. The cross around my neck. There's an image. Now I'm supposed to describe it. It's a Christian cross; it's silver and it's dirty. Dirt has collected in the cracks and it's dull and looks worn. The edges are no longer sharp; they have become round with the years.

It hangs on a silk rope that is thin and appears to be at the point of breaking. I guess I should replace it, but it feels so good around my neck. With the passing of the years I've learned to forget it's there and only briefly look upon it. It goes everywhere with me: I sleep with it, eat with it, go to school with it, go to work with it; I even take showers with it. It is never too far away from me. And I can't remember a time when I wasn't wearing it.

It's not really heavy, but it weighs enough so that I don't forget, for too long, that it's there. I don't really know why I wear it. It doesn't give me special powers; it doesn't serve as my conscience, and chances are I could go through a day perfectly fine without it. And yet I feel I need it. It doesn't do anything, really. It just hangs there, no function or duty; nothing, just hangs. And yet I feel I need it.

It reminds me of my parents; it never did before, but right now it reminds me of my parents. They are not as sharp as they used to be; they have become tired and their sharp edges have dulled with the years. I never stop thinking about them, never. If I'm at work, I worry about them. If I'm at school I wonder how their day is going. I have dreams about people hurting them. They've never really helped me with homework, because most of the time they don't understand. They don't know what I do at school or work.

See, my parents have never learned English, not because they didn't want to. They have tried many times to learn but they only have a sixth grade education. They try, but somehow it never sticks. So when we bought a house, a mortgage was like from another planet to them. Insurance, taxes, interest, someone had to take care of it. Don't get me wrong, I don't mind; I wish I could do more for them. It's like when people say, "ignorance is bliss"; they're right. I pay the bills, balance the checkbook, fill out the taxes. And it scares me. They don't have anything, except the house, and that belongs to the bank. I feel I carry them. I shouldn't have

50

to worry about all this shit for another ten years. I wish I could just not know anything and go to school and not worry about anything but school. But I feel this weight always on me, and just like the weight of the cross, I've learned to forget it's there and only briefly look upon it. I know someday I'll have to leave them. I'll have a family of my own, a mortgage of my own, and bills of my own. I also know that they will be fine without me. They will find a way to get by, the same way they got by before me. But I don't think I'll ever stop worrying about them. I don't think I'll ever stop carrying my cross.

Armando Jaquez Z.

Observe that Armando's selection of an object is off hand–but it doesn't matter. He "just happens" to pick an object full of significance, symbolic of his connection to his parents. Uncannily, his description, a detailed description, spells out that significant relationship in symbolic terms, without his awareness. (He's just fulfilling part of an assignment. But his mind has other thoughts.)

How does Armando tap into his mind's activity, the meaning of the symbolic cross? By paying attention to what his mind offers next, a life identification: "It reminds me of my parents; it never did before, but right now it reminds me of my parents."

But he goes beyond a simple life identification; he works through his description to detail the connection, and finds that the cross with its dulled edges, that "feels so good around [his] neck," that "goes everywhere" with him, that weighs him down, but not too heavily—fits perfectly as a symbol of his parents, the "cross" he carries.

The described cross becomes a *symbol* of relationship. The specific connections that Armando makes between the qualities and situation of the cross and the relationship to his parents are *metaphors*: shared likenesses, stated. Not an *actual* likeness, of course; he doesn't actually carry his parents. The cross shares *qualities* of his situation with his parents. He feels the "weight" of responsibility for them. The "sharpness" of their personalities has dulled over the years.

For now, keep a couple of useful, shorthand terms in mind. **Symbol** is the thing, place, or action itself that shares *many* qualities and situations with human life. **Metaphor** *makes* the connection to human life, one significant connection.

Why should the mind resort to images that are familiar–but so *unlike* life actually? Balloons are very different from feelings, sparrows from personal beauty and courage, and teeth from identity. The mind uses these images just because they *are* familiar, easy to visualize and easy to accept. Your life situation is likely to be more difficult to visualize, and perhaps to accept. It's hard to accept yourself as "old," and "lonely," and your life as "dismal," but less difficult to sympathize with the old woman across the street. It is hard to see that your husband has taken something out of you personally, but not so hard to entertain the image of missing teeth. Hard to keep the thought that you are both beautiful and tough in face of the coming "winter"—but not hard to entertain the image of beautiful winter sparrows.

Hard to see and accept that your long-contained feelings are getting loose–but a little less difficult to entertain a dream of balloons escaping from a black box. And perhaps it's a little unsettling to realize that as much as you love and are loved by your immigrant parents, they are your cross to bear. The mind uses symbolic images to give unfamiliar, perhaps uncomfortable, ideas a familiar, more comfortable form.

This holds for *any* object, scene, or action that draws your attention.

The following entry begins with a description of "one of those dreary days," the rain "driving [the writer, a woman] crazy."

> *So now I stare out of the window, and wonder about my chances. My chances, now that I'm on my own. I did, after all, leave my group yesterday. Kicked myself out into the world. Alone. I wonder, then, if I can make it out there.*
>
> *This day is not lending me any encouragement. There are virtually no clouds, only patches of grey against what used to be bright, blue sky. Slow mist intermittently covers the ground then disappears. The water drops left from the last mist roll down the kitchen window. Big, silent tears. Too many.*

In the identification of water drops with tears, she's already begun to make a metaphor out of her description. Next she just "notices [her] garden." But everything rides on her notice of the garden; her mind is already directing the writing process.

> *I notice my garden as I continue to stare out of the rain-soaked window. It is empty now. Long-since pulled up and prepared for winter. The ground is flat and level, waiting patiently to begin again. Still it is barren and cold. Probably frozen now underneath the surface.*

What does she notice? "It is empty now." So is her life. Her growing self, her "garden," "long-since pulled up and prepared for winter," is facing a "dormant" and "cold" spell.

But the next thought that occurs to her begins to suggest another "season" in her life. Is she aware of this? Probably not—but she soon will be. Though the ground is "barren and cold," and "probably frozen now underneath the snow," she writes that it is "waiting patiently to begin again." A metaphor is suggested here: she, also, is waiting patiently to begin again. She doesn't make this metaphor, and may not be aware yet that the writing suggests it; but the next thought that occurs to her, an imagination of spring, strongly suggests that she's close to making the connections to her life. (And she is.)

I think of what is yet to be. The spring. The host of flowers that will cover this cold, hard patch of land. Bright yellow daffodils; gleaming, red tulips; and some precious purple crocuses will rise up out of this ugly dirt, and take over. Next spring they will smile back at me when I sit at this perch and look out at them.

This imagination of spring occurs to her next. Given the day and her situation, her mind certainly had other options–but took this one. She imagines in vivid detail what will happen to that garden with the coming of spring. In the process she is also imagining herself. Those beautiful flowers "will rise up out of this ugly dirt, and take over. . . . smile back at [her]" when she looks at them again. Determined flowers, aren't they. She has a powerful image of hope, and her determination. And she's about to make the connection to her life.

Now that I look back at this entry I realize that it is not a simple reflection of my mood at the time. It is a reflection, in many ways, of how I see myself and my life. I have recently been asserting my independence. I have broken away from my parents, left my support group, and decided to give some time away from a relationship I had been pursuing. Hence, the aloneness in this image. Each time I leave something behind, even if that's a good thing, I am frightened. Unsure of the future without that person or thing.

It seemed just a couple months ago that everything was beautiful, a bright, blue sky; everything was going so well. Yes, perhaps it still is, but my life is changing again. Growing. With each change there is some darkness. Fear. There is, though, the promise of spring, and what is yet to be.

S.

The following journal entry recorded a dream of giving birth–to capital letters. (This is the author of the writings involving pulled teeth, winter sparrows, and a black box.)

I am in a hospital delivery room on a table, giving birth. There are a man and a woman at my feet. No one else in the room. The man is on my left, the woman on my right. I am partially anesthetized, dopey, but nevertheless in great pain. I cannot cry out because I am drugged. Then suddenly all of these letters come out of me. Capital letters. They are so sharp! The man and the woman are helping to pull them out of me, and it hurts, it hurts! But they are wonderful letters; I am very proud and the man and woman are congratulatory. I seem to remember only three of the middle letters--an O and two Ns, all linked together. I wish I could remember the others but the dream fades. (Perhaps it spells "noon.")

Cynthia

When you've got a dream or imagination without obvious connections to your life, locating meaning may prove difficult, especially so if the image is very unlike life, even bizarre. In that case you've got two options (at least). The first option is to take a stab at life identification, some situation that's *like* the situation of the image, or shares qualities with it. Cynthia takes this option, identifying the dream letters with her writing, which makes sense, since she is in a writing class, and the dream is about letters. "The letters, I'm sure, represent the journal I'm keeping." Label this the "life identification" option.

Making a life identification is both good and bad. It may immediately open up meaning, but it may be wrong and throw you off track. So if you make a life identification, especially a quick one, you've got try it out to see if it really fits with the *entire* image–and with your life. Cynthia tests her life identification with the entire image, and doing so confirms its validity.

The writing process has been going well, but has at times been very painful. Old issues are surfacing–things I thought were buried long ago. In the dream I like the letters and I'm proud of them even though they've hurt me. This is true about my journal; I feel that even though I have to deal with painful issues, my writing has improved a lot. It is going through a birth of sorts. A new beginning. The people in the dream are two who have helped me with this. These two people help to draw out of me something I've created within myself. I think that says it all. Lastly the anesthetic is the love I have for doing this. I enjoy writing so much that it tempers all the hard work and pain of it. For me it's definitely worth the trouble.

Cynthia

Capital letters are identified with her journal; her journal writing "has been going well," and she's "proud" of her writing. But she doesn't leave it there; she tests this identification by making metaphors of the qualities shared by the dream and her life. The capital letters are painful; in her journal she's dealing with "painful issues." Her writing is "going through a birth of sorts," a "new beginning." (The metaphor of birth is a *pun*, a metaphor with a name attached.)

She makes an identification of the two persons attending the birth with two persons who have helped her with her writing. But she doesn't leave it with those simple identifications–which always leaves the meaning yet to be realized.. And she doesn't go on to talk about these assistants—which would abort her meaning. She makes the metaphor, and applies to her life what these persons are doing in the dream: "These two people help to draw out of me something I've created within myself."

So don't make the simple life identification mistake. You'll abort your meaning and put yourself back at the beginning: the *actual* happening, place, or person, that's all. The image is trying to make the actual, *meaningful*.

54

As you work with some of your descriptions, no meaning may suggest itself, and no life identification may come to mind. In these cases, you can begin by simply talking with the image–but in personal, human terms, assuming that your mind, before long, will suggest meaning.

The following writing describes an encounter with a moth and the meaning drawn from it. A moth? Seems an unlikely *human* subject, doesn't it?

> *Bugs on my paper! I thought he was a mosquito and tried to squash him–but he's not–and now I find him welcome. Ants and gnats--all welcome. And a soft, furry moth–a small moth, my favorite color, a light beige-grey with a brush for a mouth and gold-tipping on the end of his wings and gold-brushed legs. He's completely content on my hand–lets me transfer him from hand to hand with no fear. What an odd feeling–almost a sharing, a rapport–with a bug! I don't know how he feels. I feel quite content to keep him here.*
>
> *Joan H.*

Joan begins her exploration of meaning, her talk with the image, by questioning why she chose to write about the moth–with an entire campus stretching before her. Then she explores the situation, and the quality, of that encounter in personal terms. Before long (no surprise) *human* encounters present themselves.

> *Why did I write about the moth, when there was a whole campus before me? Because he came over to me–touched me–was not afraid of me. Was close, intimate–more so than anyone else at that moment. Trusted me–seemed to like to be right there, where he was. As I reread I feel again the wonder. I felt touched, blessed, with a rare kind of closeness. Rare at any level–all too rare, I'm afraid, between people. Would that closeness between people could happen so easily, so simply–that each of us could trust–and that each trust could be repaid with the same wonder, the same gentle touching–that each of us could look–really look–at the other and find each unique, special.*
>
> *Joan H.*

Observe that as Joan questions and discusses her description, the metaphors develop quite naturally. She never makes a *specific* connection to her own life, though that connection is implied. That's fine. And not until she's halfway through the paragraph does she make a general connection with human life: " . . . a rare kind of closeness. Rare at any level—all too rare, I'm afraid, between people." Then, having made the connection, the metaphor, she thinks about human closeness using her experience with the moth. (This kind of metaphor is called an *analogy,* an extended, reasoned comparison.)

When the life connection doesn't present itself right off, just begin to talk with your image in personal, human terms; perhaps, as Joan does, with questions. Get to know the image. Life-related meaning will emerge.

Along with life identifications, the good and the bad, another problematic feature of images often presents itself: persons. When the imaged person is someone you actually know, the temptation will be to make the identification and leave it at that, thinking you have your meaning. You won't; you'll have a life identification, period. Or, you'll want to go off discussing the actual person, perhaps experiences you've had with them. It won't get you anywhere, certainly not to your meaning. Your image is still symbolic; your real-life person, like a character in a play or a film, serves as a type, illustrating certain qualities of human behavior (probably yours). This may be true even if the individual is close to you personally. Persons in your images who are *not* close to you–your long dead aunt, the President, historical figures and such–are certainly acting as characters in your image drama (most likely some version of yourself).

In the following description of a dream, the writer deals rather well with her dream persons.

I must have been nervous to go back to work today because my dreams last evening were almost nightmarish. I dreamt that I came back to work and my desk was left a mess. I was feeling very angry because people had not respected my property. Drawers were left open, papers were all over the desk top, half-filled glasses of water and mugs of coffee had been left to collect dust and mold. My calculator, tape dispenser, stapler and roll-o-dex were toppled over, not in a row as I like them to be. It was a disaster.

After seeing the mess, I stalked off down the hall for coffee only to run into the President, Anthony B. himself. He questioned me concerning my whereabouts the week before. I explained to him how I had been ill with parasites and had a bad reaction to the antibiotics. I was growing more and more nervous, and almost appeared to shrink; he grew larger and loomed over me as he spoke. He appeared not to believe a word I said. He barked at me. "Get to work and screen my calls." Lilly, his secretary, would be on vacation for the next two weeks.

I ran to my desk almost in tears; my work mate, Barbie, was there barking directions at me. "Type this proposal and conference report." She seemed to be angry that she'd had to do my job the entire week before.

I left the office angry, mad and ready to kill someone.

When I awoke I was in a bad mood and dreaded going to work that day. Thank God, all my worst fears only came true in my dream and not in reality.

Ginny G.

Look at that last comment. I've mentioned that when the image is life-like (like actual life) it's easy to make a quick, life identification and assume that you have your meaning: Ginny seems to be saying that things *at work* are actually going to be a mess when she returns, just as they were in her dream.

But as she began to search the meaning of her dream, something other than a messy desk and demanding office mates emerged, something *intangibly* messy and upsetting.

This dream really brings out two problems I've recently been struggling with in my life: fear of failure and disapproval from others and from myself regarding my job.

The dream opens with me returning to work after being out ill. I find my desk left in disarray. This indicates the disarray of my feelings concerning my career at the time I became ill and had this dream. I'm in a dead-end job with little satisfaction or prestige, in a field I no longer wish to be in. I feel I'm failing because I've only been in this position nine months and have moved from job to job in the past seven years.

The half-filled glasses are my half-filled dreams of success and happiness at work. The mold and dust indicate that I'm getting older and that time is passing.

Stalking down the hall, I run into the President. He questions me about my whereabouts, just as my father used to question me about my plans, career wise, when I lived at home. I'd explain my plans to my father, feeling like a little kid. My father would look at me as if I had no idea what I was doing. I would get more and more nervous as I tried to explain myself, as I did in the dream attempting to explain my illness to the President.

When I shrank (in the dream) I became a child and the President grew larger, becoming my father, scolding and disapproving of my career path.

The President's barking orders were actually my father's. He used to bark directions as to what he thought would be best for me to do career wise, making me feel that my ideas were worthless and that I was a failure.

Running from my desk, as I would run from my father's disapproval, I was only confronted with more barking of directions from Barbie. I realize that I can't escape or run away from the fear of failure; someone will always offer direction and disapproval of my life. I think that's why I awoke feeling angry. I felt hopeless. Now I look back and realize that I can work on dealing with it myself. I'm starting to come to terms with these problems in my life, and I realize I can only do my best. Someone will always disapprove of my life no matter how much I try, but I still am haunted by it.

Ginny G.

In exploring the meaning of the dream, Ginny has come to terms with something beyond her problems with the President and her father; she's dealing with an entire theme or pattern in her life.   Yes, the actual situation with the President is part of it.   So is the situation with her father, whatever remains of it.   But the problem of others directing and disapproving of her applies to her entire life, and has become one of its themes.

Keep open the range of possible meanings as you explore your descriptions. The meaning may locate in one specific situation; it may locate in lots of places in your life; or it may apply as a theme to your entire life in some respect.

As you read the following dream and its interpretation, keep in mind what's been discussed: that searching for meaning is to tap what your mind does naturally, that your mind, naturally, will assist you in the process; that a simple life identification–left at that–will abort your meaning; that a life identification may also distort meaning unless you can make it work with the *entire* image; and that persons in your images, even those close to you, are most likely acting as characters, as if in a drama.

> *I am running down a long corridor. Someone is chasing me. A man. Not threatening, but I want to get away. I see a door open on the left and I run into a room. The man follows me and locks the door. I am trapped. I'm in an old apartment hotel, the kind I used to live in for a while. My room is a tiny efficiency apartment, comfortable, but <u>so</u> small. Attractive wallpaper the color of summer grass. White woodwork, thick with years of paint. Opposite the first door, a second. White. The bathroom. I run inside and lock the door. I am relieved: Now <u>I</u> am in control.*
>
> *I look for a way to escape. The bathroom window is really small, a modern crank window, with a metal frame around each pane. Even if I broke the glass, I could never fit through. I look out the window. I'm on the top floor of an old red brick building. The roof slopes steeply from beneath the window, all the way down to the fourth or fifth floor. (I'm about 20 stories up.) If I can slide down the roof, perhaps I'll survive the last long drop.*
>
> *The man outside the door turns into J. (my husband). He calls out, asking if I'm O.K. I say no, that I'm sick because he has frightened me. I tell him I'll be out soon. I look through my purse; I need something to use as a screwdriver. The window has changed to one large pane of glass. If I can unscrew it around the edges I'll be free! I work on it.*
>
> *J. says something again and I open the door a little. The room outside has changed to a deep rose color. There's a lamp glowing warmly in the corner. J. looks past me and sees my purse on the windowsill. He knows what I've been doing. He pretends he doesn't. I close and lock the door again.*

58

I get the windowpane out. But now the roof slopes only a little and then drops off 17 or 18 stories. I would be killed instantly. No escape after all.

I open the door and return to the outside room. For some reason I have been unable to replace the windowpane. J. sees what I've been up to, but still pretends he doesn't know. We sit down and play a game of cards. The door to the corridor is still locked but I have given up trying to get out. For now.

Though this is a long, complex dream, the writer, Cynthia, goes at it detail by detail, thoroughly exploring the entire image for meaning. She gets a load of meaning for her troubles, an understanding of just where she is in her marriage, what drove her there, and what the future holds. (This is the writer of the pulled teeth, sparrows, black box, and the birthing of capital letters. These images, which she just happened to record in her journal, work a theme.)

As you read note the metaphors made, and the metaphors with puns, often put in quotes to suggest the special meaning made by the pun.

The main idea here is that I feel trapped in a situation (my marriage) but I'm unable to escape at present. The image begins in a corridor, a "passage" of some sort for me, in an old brick apartment hotel. The building looks sturdy, secure, traditional (as my life most likely appears from the outside), but houses something transient. I am in transit, moving, being chased into a room on the left, some situation that is not "right." In a sense I felt chased into marriage with J.; I wasn't sure at the time he was the "right" person or that I was making the "right" decision. The image seems to confirm this. This building is of a type I "used to live in for a while," suggesting that I can exist, but not live, there now.

The room itself appears pleasant, "comfortable." The marriage is "comfortable," financially very comfortable, but "small," confining; I have no "space."

The wallpaper is green, like summer grass. Green is the color of growth, but this "growth" is paper thin, and only hides the walls. In my marriage I am allowed a thin layer, a tiny amount, of personal growth, but beyond that I am limited. The growth of the relationship is limited. The "white" woodwork is "thick with years of paint"—years of "painting" everything "white," of whitewashing all the problems.

The bathroom is my private space, where I retreat emotionally and "lock the door." It has a "window" to see "outside" the marriage. But I can't escape through it; the way is blocked by the metal window frame and two metal strips or bars dividing the window, just as escape from my marriage is barred by my two children. Even if I break through whatever insulates me from the outside world, the two bars still keep me from escaping.

The sloped roof confuses me. I'd say the last four or five floors represent the last years of the marriage—the four or five years left until A. is in school full

59

time. The long drop I believe refers to the financial "fall" I'm going to take if I divorce J.

The screwdriver is a tool to help me escape; I'm trying to "unscrew" something. (As sexual symbolism that's pretty funny, and very close to the truth.)

J. tries to communicate something to me, so I open the door a little (to my private space). Now the room is rose colored, "rosy," and the light is on. J. understands what's going on but pretends everything is "rosy."

When I finally "get the pane out," or perhaps get the pain *out, I see that the drop is steeper than I imagined. Seventeen or eighteen stories. The escape from my marriage will not be long and easy like the sloping roof, but a quick drop and a long fall for the seventeen or eighteen years until my kids are adults.*

J. sees my "purse"—my bags, my "luggage" perhaps—on the window sill. He knows that I'm ready to go. The sad part of all this is that I'm sure he does *know, he just refuses to acknowledge it, as he refuses to acknowledge the problems in our marriage. So we go back to playing a game of cards (in a house of cards), pretending everything is OK.*

Cynthia

Though these writings work with meaning *following* the description, you may get into a writing where image and meaning develop quite naturally in concert. Let that happen. The following writing is of that sort.

I saw something yesterday that disturbed me very much. I drive past General Mills on my way to school in the morning, and then again on my way home. On my way to school yesterday morning I noticed that demolition of the old place had begun. As I slowly drove by, I saw for the first time that a crane with a wrecking ball attached to it had begun to smash the front loading dock.

Since last April 28, when I worked my final day at General Mills, after spending almost 20 years of my life there, I've had the opportunity to view the plant, a boxy seven-story red brick structure, during daylight hours and at night. Since then, nothing has seemed different about the plant. The "only" thing different was that I didn't work there anymore. Nobody did. The whole place is dormant now. The lucky 50 employees who remain, work in the new, state-of-the-art addition next door waiting for the axe to one day fall on them. Even though the old building sits idle now and has since April, every time I've driven past, things didn't look all that different, except for the number of cars parked in the parking lot.

But yesterday was different. Much different. Yesterday I saw death. All the lights are out now. The building where I spent almost 20 years of my life, the building that I used to call my "second home," is just cold and empty and dark. They've turned all the lights out. Forever. They've turned out the lights on the lives of so many people. The people I grew to know and love. And sometimes

60

hate. Doesn't matter. I forgive them all. All the people I disliked or distrusted for whatever reason. All's forgotten. The building still remains though, but soon it will be reduced to rubble. All that remains are the memories. There have been so many wonderful people I've had the pleasure to have known, people I used to share meals with, get drunk with, and party with. I think about them all and sometimes wish it could have gone on forever. But nothing lasts forever, except for the memories that I now carry with me. They are indelibly etched into my memory and are tucked safely away in the sub consciousness of my mind.

But let me tell you something. Seeing that building today has evoked some pretty heavy emotions. Anger. Abandonment. Fear. And tears. I cried like a baby in my wife's arms the day I found out I was losing my job. I still find myself shedding a tear now and then. I cry as I write in this journal; and I cried again when I saw how the wrecking ball was starting to destroy the place where I had labored so long.

In the days and weeks to come, more and more of the building, which stood proud and strong for over 70 years, will soon disappear for good. I will serve as a witness to that slow death every day as I leave for school and again as I come back home in the evening. I feel as if a part of me "dies" every time I see that place. Everyone seems to come to grips over the death of a loved one, and so too will I recover from this death as well.

J. Truby

The author has lost his job along with many others. On his way to college, where he's retraining, he has passed the old work place, now dormant, many times. But this time something is different; the wrecking ball is at work. He only mentions that fact, then goes back in time to describe the building as it was after he lost his job; apparently nothing much changed, just fewer cars in the lot, the building unused for the most part.

But the wrecking ball is at work and the lights are out (the metaphors are obvious). Suddenly the reality of his loss hits him full force. With that realization he spells out the symbolic implications: "Yesterday I saw death. All the lights are out now. . . . They've turned all the lights out. Forever. . . . on the lives of so many people." He sees the destruction of the building as a symbol, and begins to draw out the metaphors.

> *. . . the building . . . will soon disappear for good. I will serve as a witness to that slow death every day as I leave for school and again as I come back home in the evening. . . . a part of me "dies" every time I see that place.*

Back and forth, between description and its implications, he develops the meaning of his experience. Realizing the symbolic implications in the destruction

61

of his old workplace, he can think more concretely about what has happened, and feel its full impact.

His writing captures that impact, closely following his awareness of what he is observing. Though the writing is reflective and thoughtful, his thinking is tied closely to concrete experience. When you've got a writing in which the meaning unfolds as you write, by all means do what you can to keep it unfolding.

Suggested Writings:

As you go about your life, what scenes arrest your attention, especially with more than usual feeling? Stop. Take time to describe the scene. In the description you will find more than you saw at first glance.

Look over your most vivid, feeling-filled descriptions (whether actual scenes, events, imaginations, or dreams). Ask yourself what meanings might be there. Opposite the description (on the left-hand page of your journal) write out your thoughts. Assume that the image is symbolic: that the situation described in the image is like some situation in your life at present. Detail by detail, scene by scene, write what the image seems to be showing and saying to you about your life at present, or about the past as it impacts the present.

Within these writings you might find the seeds of a sketch, a poem, a short essay, a story (from actual life or imagined), or a short dramatic piece: a monologue, a dialogue, or perhaps a scene. These explorations of meaning may also lead into an essay or memoir, which Chapter 6 will discuss more fully.

"Depressing Subjects"—impact and action:

In reading through the book, some have commented on the "depressing" content of some entries, whether it is necessary to write pieces like these. I tell them that the subject is wide open, but that entries like these more than occasionally get written when the subject *is left op*en, and writers are encouraged to describe *whatever* they are drawn to, and to record their memories, imaginations and dreams.

But that doesn't quite account for the frequency with which "depressing" stuff gets written. Something is at work here, which has to do with the nature of writing as it relates to experience. Experiential writing that matters most usually springs from an impact: a destructive relationship, the loss of a loved one, a setback, a trauma, the crush of some circumstance, or a big change in circumstance (going off to college, changing jobs, or relocating).

These impacts stimulate writing, and find their way into descriptions that weren't intended to be about them at all, because with writing the mind constructs its own version of the impacts, first to make the impacts visible—but then to turn them around.

The mind acts on the impacts, infusing these images with its own vitality, vitality that counters the impacts, encouraging life to emerge.

62

You have seen this sequence of impact and action again and again in the writings you've read; you will see it in the essays that follow. And you have heard, and will hear, writers comment on it.

L*ife* is emerging with these "depressing" writings, which makes them something else. The mind is acting and planning action to counter and rework the impacts. It's an old, very human story, not the all too familiar story of human tragedy, but "tragedy" understood in time, reworked—and sometimes stood on its head. What's depressing?—*ignoring images offered by the mind.*

Cynthia (of the several descriptions and interpretations in this chapter) reviewing months of image-exploration, writes:

Then came the work of drawing meanings from images, and the realization that everything I'd written meant something—something vital to me personally. With practice I learned to draw out the qualities of my experience, my images, my dreams, and find in them significant expression of, and comment on, my actual, present life. Symbol. Metaphor. Meaning.

My confining marriage was clearly represented in dreams of a black box and a locked hotel room. The fear and misery of a contemplated divorce was evident in images of rain, of winter, of a fall from a 20-story building. My mind, through my journal, was taking stock of my problems. But not only problems. New ideas presented themselves: choices, encouragements. Hope. Hints of a re-awakening self emerged in a "Sleeping Beauty" entry. Images of lovers reunited in the rain, of birds surviving the winter gave me insights into a newly reconciled, resilient self, a self that could cope with adversity. The knowledge of this inner strength would help me greatly in the year that followed.

And for a final note on depressing subjects—

. . . it's important to make a lot of the highs in life and show great respect for the lows. I need to understand why there's been pain. As much as I, like most others, would prefer not to experience life's painful moments, attempting to ignore them deprives me of the intense feelings that only we as human beings are capable of.

Donna

63

Symbols and Sets of Symbols:
getting familiar with the "forgotten language"

The explorations for meaning read so far might serve as a short, sketchy introduction to symbolism, suggesting a very few symbols within the range of possibilities–which are enormous. All of literature and all of the arts worldwide illustrate something of that range. And as individuals, each of us has a set of symbols both from humanity's common storeroom, and from our very own. (The "forgotten language," by the way, is the psychologist Eric Fromm's term.)

The reason symbols are both humanity's acommon property and our own is found in the purpose of symbols. Using images from the common, familiar stuff of our lives, the mind makes the unfamiliar in human life familiar: the nature of a fear, a perception, or desire; the quality or situation of the self, or of a relationship, or group interaction. We share in common life experience with the rest of the human race, so we share common symbols. We also have experiences that are unique, cultural and individual. A German shepherd in one person's image might symbolize friendship or loyalty; in another's (someone who has been attacked by dogs) it might symbolize threat or aggression. But in our experiences of phenomena like day and night, winter and summer, mountains and valleys, lakes and deserts we share much with the rest of humanity, and have produced commonly shared symbols.

Nothing so engages our minds as does the question: what is it to be a human self in the company of other humans and within the natural world? It is the subject of all the arts, including the recently created arts of film and photography.

Let's explore a few common symbols. Hopefully you'll become more acutely aware of the symbols your mind uses to construct its images, and why.

Bodies: We are more familiar with our own bodies than any object on earth. Not surprisingly, our language and thinking are full of body symbolism: we shoulder a load, get gut feelings, have heart, get a head start, a foot in the door, make elbow room, butt in.

Persons: We're very familiar with certain types of persons, family members for sure. So, if the mind needs a fatherly, motherly, childlike or grand-motherly *character* for an image, what better persons to use than your own, very familiar (notice the metaphor in "familiar") family. This should be a caution–against literal interpretations–when family members appear in your images. They may be themselves, especially if something is going on currently between you and them. But they may function simply as a type or character. The image of your very aggressive brother may be the image of your own aggressive self. You're so *familiar* with your brother's personality that it's perfect for making you familiar with yourself.

64

What characteristics of self or your human relations might royal figures, presidents, authorities, or lawmen have? What's your familiarity with these figures?

Animals: The animal kingdom carries a symbolism we're very familiar with and often use in conversation. We apply animal names like cat, dog, snake, rat, bug, bull, and bear to human beings and human situations without a second thought. So it isn't surprising that animals frequently show up in mental images, suggesting something of our animal selves: our appetites, instincts, and emotions.

Plant Life: A dominant symbolism of the plant kingdom is captured in images of blossoming and growth, or withering and decay. Human life, like plant life, needs a "ground" to grow from, "light," nurture; and, like plant life, it is especially vulnerable during early growth. What different symbolic qualities might a potted plant and a tree exhibit? A meadow and a forest? Roots or blossoms? Seeds?

Dwellings and Places: Of all dwellings, we are most familiar with the house. What's a house to you? A refuge, a comfort, a prison, stability? Think of the different character of its various rooms: the living room/family room, kitchen, dining room, bathroom, bedrooms, basement, attic. Which room is the most private, which most yours? In which room do you find "warmth," good company, retreat, nourishment? In which do you store forgotten things (like memories)? Where's the "base" of this dwelling?

You get the point. The character of various parts of the house will find its way into your images when they need to show: protection, privacy, warmth, companionship, nourishment, memory, your "base," and the like.

Neighborhood and City: Beyond the family house lies the neighborhood; and beyond that the city. The symbolism isn't difficult; this is where we meet our near society, and society in general. So images of the neighborhood and city bring us our sense of society in some respect. And the countryside? Brings us something of the opposite, the individual alone in nature. (What's your experience of "country?")

The Natural World: What do the familiar features of the natural world have to offer as symbols–oceans, lakes, rivers, swamps and shorelines; hills, mountains, valleys, plains, and deserts? Think of their characteristics and qualities. Bodies of water have a visible, moving surface (sometimes agitated and stormy); and a calmer, less and less visible undersurface. (So does your mind.)

Rivers flow, most often one way; they can't back up. (So does time.) Rivers used to separate people and places (and still do).

Hills, mountains, and valleys, if you think for a minute, have obvious symbolisms. What about swamps, deserts? Have you been "swamped" lately, or found yourself "deserted," isolated, without company, "dry?"

Movements and the Journey: Movement is life; immobility, death. In that regard "going somewhere" or "not getting anywhere" has a lot to say about the disposition of a life. So it's not surprising that journeys and the journey story are symbolic of human life lived in the awareness of time. (So writes W. H. Auden in an article on Tolkien's *Lord of the Rings.)* The life-related features of the journey are these:

- Like life, the journey is usually a journey alone, from a known and familiar dwelling (family or society) into unknown and unfamiliar places.
- Like time, the journey is not reversible.
- Like life lived in time, the path or road has its choices, and they often determine a particular kind of life. (Remember Robert Frost's "The Road Not Taken"?)
- Like life, one unexpectedly encounters friends or enemies on the journey without knowing which is which.
- Like life, the destination is generally toward a new "dwelling"; or, the goal accomplished, a return home to make a new dwelling.

Movement in its widest scope, then, gives us the journey and the journey story, a sense of our lives lived in time.

Various vehicles might symbolize something of how we're making the journey at a particular time, or how we'd like to; and the power at our disposal, or desired. Imagine the different symbolic possibilities of a car, a bicycle or motorcycle, a train, an airplane, or a ship. Imagine the very different qualities of walking, running, or swimming, what these modes of locomotion would say about the journey through life.

All this seems obvious when you take a moment to think about it. And it is; these are the familiar features of our lives. But we often forget that it is just these familiar things, places, circumstances, persons, and actions that the mind employs in mental images—to give us a graphic picture of what we *don't* know, or know dimly, of our human lives. This is true, especially, of the natural world. Richard Wilbur, poet, writes that without the natural world we would know nothing of "all we mean or wish to mean." It is through this world that "we have seen ourselves and spoken."

Symbolic images also saturate the arts, so there's a double benefit of getting familiar with symbolic images; as a student, Cynthia Todd writes, ". . . plays, poetry, music, and paintings suddenly started to make sense."

A Note on Immersion:

I'm aware that I've immersed you in close readings of image after image. My hope is that you will recall and relearn the "forgotten language," and become convinced of its importance. Modern society doesn't make much room for this. But the mind does.

There's more to come; get used to it, if you will. The drama is only half over.

66

5 WORKING ESSAYS OF THE JOURNAL

At first, your journal may have seemed to be mostly about persons, events, objects and scenes other than yourself or your life. But it's clear by now, isn't it, that your journal concerns—you, your experience. The more you explore your descriptions for meaning, the clearer this personal focus will become. It's always the case. Joan Didion, in a famous essay about journals ("On Keeping a Notebook"), imagines that her notebook is about *other* people. "But," she writes, "of course it is not."

And shouldn't be. Scores of writers remind us that personal experience, the self, is the right place for a writer to begin. The father of the essay, Montaigne, whose topics ranged the world, writes, "Thus, reader, I am myself the matter of my book." Henry Thoreau, with a little humor thrown in, writes:

In most books, the I, or first person, is omitted; in this it will be retained . . . it is, after all, always the first person that is speaking. I should not talk so much about myself if there were anybody else whom I knew as well. Unfortunately, I am confined to this theme by the narrowness of my experience. Moreover, I, on my side, require of every writer, first or last, a simple and sincere account of his own life . . .

And James Baldwin writes: "One writes out of one thing only—one's own experience."

Realizing that your journal concerns yourself, it may seem that your journal entries are just miscellaneous. That's unlikely, strange as it may seem. Your mind, more likely, has been essaying without your awareness.

This shouldn't seem strange. The journal requires no particular subject; it's wide open to *whatever* your mind might care to explore. With the journal, then, your mind has a playing field to try out and test its images and ideas—to essay.

Images and ideas on a particular life situation may be scattered through your journal, they may be clumped together, you may find them in the neighborhood of an entry where you are dealing at length with some issue in your life—or you may find that you have a rough essay developing, entry by entry, as you write journal entries. This may be obvious; it may take some searching, but you may surprise yourself with what you find.

67

The first of the two essays that follow uses three images from the writer's journal. As she worked with them she found that they not only developed a significant theme, but led her essay in an unexpected direction—and gave her control of her subject matter in more ways than one.

When I first began writing this essay I thought it would be about how my parents control my life. About how I was stuck in a situation I felt hopeless in. I felt there was no way out; there was nothing I could do. I was wrong. I started to think about the three images I was going to work with. I thought about them long and hard. Slowly, I began to realize how they escalated from being depressing to being something I actually enjoy. I began to see how my parents used to control my life and how they control it now. After comparing the two, it dawned on me that without even realizing it, I had the control in _my_ hands. The control they have over me now is only physical: They still tell me I can't go here or I can't do this. In the past they also controlled me mentally and emotionally. They told me what their idea of right and wrong was and I wasn't to disagree. What they thought I should do with my life, what their idea of proper and improper was. They controlled my every thought.

Now it's different. Even though they may still control me physically, their control over me mentally has been broken. I have a mind of my own, which I am quite proud of. I'm not sure how or when it happened, but to my own personal enjoyment, it alarms my parents. Their game plan for me has been shattered. I have shattered it with the personal growth they never thought I would, or could, achieve. They expected me to grow up like most well-brought-up Greek girls. Get good grades in school, maybe go on to college, then meet an equally well-brought-up Greek boy, settle down and get married. For a long time during my high school years I believed it was the right thing also. I had no direction, no game plan of my own. But now I do have one. A good one. I want to become a successful attorney, something my parents are afraid of but also ignore. They are afraid because they think it will ruin my chances for marriage considerably. Who will want me at age 26 or 27? They ignore it because they truly believe I will never make it that far. Somewhere along the way some Greek Romeo is going to sweep me off my feet and carry me off into the sunset, leaving any of my silly ideas behind.

Three images have helped me with this; each have their own separate and distinct meaning, but come together to form a whole picture. The first image had the most impact on me because I never understood what it meant until I saw it on paper. It started occurring at a very difficult time in my life. It was hard enough being 15 and my parents surely didn't make it any easier. In the dream I am in a wheelchair. My mother is standing in front of me, smiling. I try to speak to her, but my voice comes out only in a very soft whisper. I try to move my wheelchair but it won't go; I try to get up but my legs won't move. My mother starts to walk away from me and I frantically try to get her attention. I pound my fists on the chair and I try to scream, but I can't. I remember such a feeling of helplessness that I've

68

never had before. I couldn't do anything to grab her attention or make her listen to me.

In this image my immobility and the wheelchair represent a lot. On one hand the chair represents the fact that my parents want me to stay put—not go anywhere. Stay home and be a good little girl by their standards. On the other hand it represents my inability to "budge" from the situation; I was only 15, what could I do? There was no one around at that time to help me "get out of the wheelchair" and get me moving. I was "stuck." My inability to speak is the part of the image that is most painful to me. In the dream I'm trying to speak to my mother but my voice is so weak she can't hear me. I try to call out to her but she turns her back on me. This part of the image has a very literal meaning. My mother has always "heard" what I've said but has never "listened." To her, I was just a teenager; what did I know? Only she knew what was best for me, even if it did hurt me. My "voice" in most matters didn't account for anything. She thought that all the pain she caused would be forgotten sooner or later anyway. Eventually, up until a year or so ago, the dream stopped occurring. I didn't question why. I was glad it was gone. It bothered me too much. But now I see why it doesn't occur anymore. It's because I am no longer "stuck" in that wheelchair. I am mobile. My thoughts and ideas now come and go as they please.

The second image, "the wedding" was more reassuring because I was more in control. I saw myself in a wedding dress, getting ready to be married. My mother was nagging me to hurry up; the ceremony was at noon and I wasn't even ready yet. I remember feeling depressed; I didn't want to get married.

This image was easier to interpret. The time of the wedding holds the entire symbolism. In Greek weddings a noon ceremony is unheard of because it's too early in the day. If I would get married at the time my mother would like it would be "too early" in my life, in my opinion. I would feel "rushed." I want to finish school first and establish a career. I want to live my own life before I go from one commitment (my parents) to another (husband).

The third image is my personal favorite. I am in total control and in the position I would like to be in a few years. I am a powerful attorney cross-examining a witness. My questions are smart and my manner cut-throat. After my questioning is through, I go back to my desk. A man is sitting there, an old professor from law school. He praises my work and raves about what a great lawyer I am. I feel wonderful, radiant. This image is the most literal. I am finally in control, in the image, and in my life. I see myself where I want to be and doing what I want to do. No parents, no pressure. Just a feeling of accomplishment and happiness.

These three images, when put together, show the stages of my personal development, almost like a time line. The first image, which began years ago, was of a smaller child struggling to be heard, struggling for some control. The second image, which came years later, is of a person beginning to make up her own mind and making decisions for herself despite fierce opposition. The third image, the most recent one, is of a person who has worked hard and has let nothing get in the way of what she wants.

I now realize how much I have grown as a person. I have moved away from the person my parents want me to be, and have begun a new life for myself. A life with direction; and a life that is entirely up to me, for a change.

F. D

She finished her paper with this comment concerning its writing:

If I hadn't started writing this paper, I would never have seen that it <u>was</u> really for me. I would never have realized how much I have broken away from my parents. Maybe not the way I thought I would have, by moving out, but in the way part of me already has.

". . . the way part of me already has." The essay of journal materials is a fine means to find out just what sort of essaying your mind has already accomplished.

Notice the framework of her paper: She begins with an idea that she seems somewhat sure of: that her parents control her life, and how hopeless that situation is. Her assumption was that their *impact* was the whole picture. But her three images have captured more than impact; they have captured a vital process well under way: *She* has begun to take control of her life. But she had to think "long and hard" about her images to realize what has already been established in her mental life.

She continues, using her images one at a time to show just what sort of mental control she has gained, and is gaining, over her life. Observe what close attention she pays to the particular features of the images as she translates their meanings to her life.

In this thinking-writing process, observe: *she lets that original idea change*—significantly. That's crucial with the working essay, which is a process of trying and testing an idea against images and thoughts the mind brings to bear upon it.

Finally, and simply, she sums up; and after that summing up voices her clear realization. Note that now and then she comments on the writing/thinking process, which is common with essays.

The following essay is also written with reference to a journal. In the essay a woman deals with dominant figures in her life for the first time.

*If you had asked me three months ago how my life was, I would have spelled it with bold, capital letters. **BORING.** But after a few journal entries, I began to realize that my life is not boring after all. In fact, it is a wealth of experiences I*

70

never realized I had until I started writing them one by one. A blizzard of emotions comes back as if it were only yesterday. What a change it has had on me. The way I view things now is quite different from the way I saw things before. It opened my eyes to what life really means.

The traumatic experiences I've had, I see them as the major challenges in my life. The death of my mother is one of them. I remember especially that cold, dreary day when Mom was buried. The cemetery was packed with relatives and friends and we all held hands around the grave while the coffin was being brought down. That was the hardest part. Knowing that I would never see her again. I realized then that even if my tears were buckets-full, I would never be able to bring her back. I had lost someone special to me, someone to whom I owe my life.

At that particular moment I realized: That's it; she's gone, and she's never coming back. What a great impact that experience had on me. I never occurred to me that mom could actually die. Her death brought me to the realization that life is so short and precious. That life should not be taken for granted. That life is something we have to be thankful for. I surely opened my eyes to the real meaning of life.

Mom's death was an eye opener. But there was still something holding me back, something that just wouldn't let go . . . until I began to see images, images that somehow related to my current situation. In one of the images I imagined a mother looking out the window with teary eyes and a child waving her hand and saying goodbye. The child continues walking forward until she is out of sight. Then everything turns white.

This image represents a whole lot to me. It symbolizes me (the child in the image) bidding my final farewell to grieving for mom. I realize that unless I let go of these feelings, unless I say goodbye to all the hurts and pains caused by her death unless I realize that there is more to life than death—then it would always hold me back. Her death has caused me so much pain and sorrow, but I can no longer grieve—for I already have. I want to remember mom more for the time when she was alive rather than dead, because her spirit still dwells within me. Her presence will always be felt till I myself am no longer here on earth.

Although that was a difficult time, I discovered an important ingredient in life— courage. Courage to face the situation or problem head on. Without courage I never would have made it. I never would have been able to face a new day with new insights and a new perspective on life.

I must admit that courage doesn't come with a flick of a finger. It comes as a learning experience. At times, in fact most of the time, I feel like a coward myself. It is only lately that I realized that a courageous person doesn't have to have a black belt tied to their waist. The only thing one needs is a pen and paper.

Surely courage doesn't come easily. Oh yes, there are times when I feel like a wimp. And I get angry. All my life I have let other people run my life for me. My decisions, actions, and ambitions were all being influenced by other people, particularly by persons around me who I thought loved and cared for me. I didn't have the courage then to stand up for my rights. Let alone the courage to speak out.

My upbringing, I suppose, is a major factor. I was brought up in a home where "good" girls are supposed to just nod their heads and say, "yes" all the time. If I tried to reason out, my parents thought that it was a sign of disrespect. So I grew up being this "good" girl type and brought this naivety into my marriage. And I hate it! It is only lately that I have realized that I do have courage in me when I began to see images, and somehow related those images to my current situation.

In one image I see a king—a mighty and powerful one, but his kingdom is filled with discontent among the people. The king rules with an iron fist and no one dare to disobey his commands. His word is like a commandment; anyone who disobeys it will be punished.

In my image I see a slave who dares to tell the king how unhappy everyone is, including her. The king, being so hard-hearted, punishes the slave by slashing her tongue out. In great pain, but in deep anger, the slave kicks the king and he falls down from his throne. The king orders the slave's feet to be cut off, and finally she is taken out of the palace into the woods. The slave's anger does not stop there. She still has her eyes, nose, ears, hands, and mind. She still wants to fight, but she has no weapon. She starts to dig her hands into her pockets, pulls out a piece of paper, and with the blood coming out of her slashed tongue she starts to write, in pain and in agony. One by one she lists the things she dislikes about the king and when each one is done she recovers, little by little, her tongue and feet. She is now a free woman!

This image is one of my favorites because it relates to one of the most important ingredients in life—courage.

As I looked back at this image, I see the king's image as that of my husband. He rules, overpowers like a king. His word is the final, the only, word that matters. My opinion doesn't. He hears, but never really listens.

I see myself as the slave in this image. I feel like I'm being cut up into pieces. My tongue slashed—I can't tell him my ideas because it doesn't matter to him anyway. I had no other weapon except a pen and paper, and of course my hand and mind to write and think.

Getting these feelings of anger off my chest is such a relief that I consider myself a free woman, a woman who has her identity and the courage to defend herself from losing her self-respect. This image gives me a sense of relief when I feel like nobody cares and listens to what I have to say. It gives me a sense of freedom to write and say what's in my mind without anybody controlling me. I'm glad that I still do have my mind to think and my hands and fingers to communicate the deeper emotions that I have kept within me. I am free! It gives me a refreshing feeling to live freely.

I confronted my husband about his macho attitude (an attitude common to most men, I might say) because it irritated and bothered me a lot. He didn't want to admit it at first, but when I began to cite instances where his macho attitude really showed in our relationship, he finally admitted to it. He didn't realize that it was much of a problem; nor did he realize that it was upsetting me.

It might take years to unravel this attitude problem of his but I'll keep on fighting. During all twelve years of my marriage I have been very submissive to my husband. Whatever he said, went. Whatever he decided, right or wrong, was always the best no matter what the outcome was. And I was supposed to follow and just say, "amen." I was like a puppet on a string. I couldn't move without someone pulling m arms and legs; or talk without someone opening my mouth. I felt controlled. And I didn't like it at all. I don't want to be controlled any longer—not by anyone—including my husband. I want to be able to control my own life. I feel a deep sense of rebellion building up inside of me; I am ready to explode. I'm angry at him for controlling my life, and at the same time I'm angry at myself for letting him be the puppet master. I don't want to be tied to the strings any longer. I want to be free. If it will take years for him to change his macho attitude—then I'll keep on fighting until he realizes that I am his equal.

If courage is defined as one's ability to speak what's in one's mind, then I am beginning to discover that I do have courage. All the while it's been there. All it needed was to be discovered. Exploring and grasping the meaning of images helped me to realize how vital courage is in my life.

In another image about courage I see an old tree stump standing right beside a pine tree. Its branches, before it was cut down, extended a long way out. What came as a surprise to me was that underneath that huge tree was this pine tree which had experienced tremendous growth every since the huge tree had been cut down. It was amazing. The leaves of the pine tree exhibit a different color now—from chestnut brown to apple green. Now I see real growth. It used to be protected, from the scorching rays of the sun and from the rustle of the wind, by the huge elm tree. But now that the elm tree is cut down, a green pine tree emerges ready to face a new day, ready to face the scorching rays of the sun, ready to face the rain or the snow. Its growth was stunted before. Not anymore. Despite the changes in season, I see a never-ending growth, growth that won't stop no matter what. It's ready to fight good or bad weather. The pine tree opens its arms to the pouring rain and welcomes the rays of the morning sun.

Every time I looked at that pine tree I saw myself, growing emotionally and mentally. Having been the baby in the family, everything was pretty much se up for me. I had everything I could ever ask for in my life. But being this over-protected child, I noticed that I was that I was not growing emotionally and mentally. I had never been really burdened, and I had never made or been allowed to make major decisions in my life. My actions, my mood, my behavior, my ambitions were all pretty much numbered. They were controlled by other people, by what other people would think and say. I was beginning to lose an important part of me—my own *identity. When my parents died (the elm tree being cut down) I learned to live, cope and survive. The morning sun represents the future challenges in my life that I had to face, and the rain represents forgiveness to wash all the past and start anew. I am gaining new insight and new perspective, realizing that I am responsible for me and me alone.*

I had always been controlled during my upbringing and it showed up in my marriage. I am putting an end to being a puppet all my life. Looking at the pine tree, I began to realize that I am responsible for my own life, and no one else.

I admire the courage I saw in that pine tree. It is ready to fact the weather— rain or snow, just like me. No matter what adversities I might be facing in the future, I will be able to face them, because I have discovered an important tool— courage. Courage to face life head on; courage to face adversities and realize that life is more than a trial. It is an adventure. Life is not dreary; it is exciting. Life is not all sorrows; it is joy. Life is not worthless; it is precious. And life has a lot more to offer to someone like me who lives it with courage.

E. M. B.

I don't think much comment is necessary on this one, meaning spelled out as clearly as it is. But I have to say that the central image, the king-slave drama, is an image as dramatic as any I've ever read, and a (very) strong statement on the power of writing. Perhaps you observed that this working essay evolved, as essays naturally do: she got hold of her situation, took a stance, and acted

The following essay comes out of a two hundred-page journal in which all but two entries related to the author's theme. She goes deeply into her journal, mines it completely, and makes such profound realizations, she recounted later, that for three months she just had to just let it go and let the realizations settle in. (This essay might also serve as an extension of the symbol catalogue, as you will see. The author deals with dozens of images.)

The main theme of the writings in my journal is that I have recently gone through an identity crisis. Before I stayed home to have a child, my career was my whole life. McDonald's was my family for almost ten years. At McDonald's I was a star. I was important. I had power. I had my own little kingdom. I knew exactly who I was.

When I stayed at home and gave up my career, I experienced a great loss. In efforts to fill the void, I attempted to replace my McDonald's family with my biological family.

The writings in my journal, fortunately, have not only help me through the struggle of determining my identity, but have served as a catalyst in surfacing feelings toward my family, specifically in regards to my mother, which I have been suppressing for the past twenty-five years or more. Feelings that have directly affected my perspective on people, families, life in general, and most significantly

74

myself. I believe that it is only because of my awareness of the feelings towards my mother that I have been able to in fact know myself.

With the exception of two of the writings in my journal, each one in some way deals with the conflicts involved in giving up my identity in a corporate "family," and finding my identity as a new mother.

One of my very first is the Mirror image. In this writing my mind is presented as a large attic full of many boxes and trunks covered with dust and many cobwebs. The many boxes and trunks symbolize the many feelings that I have been suppressing over the years. The dust is representative of time. The many cobwebs representative of confusion and mixed feelings.

One of the most significant points in the Mirror Image writing, which clearly keys into the conflict going on within me, is the image of the red satin ribbon marking a page in a dictionary upon which are the words, "know thyself." The red satin ribbon, like a prize, is my passionate qualities. Until I know myself I'm not experiencing life to its fullest.

In the Mirror Image I saw myself in cleaning attire, babushka, jeans, and shirtsleeves rolled up. This indicates my readiness to really do some "mind cleaning." The significance of the babushka, a type I wrote, "which I never wear myself while cleaning house," is that it symbolizes a new approach to the mind cleaning. The new approach is the journal. My attempts to wipe away the cobwebs became difficult because of the heaviness of the broom. The broom's weight represents the gravity and seriousness of the task and the burdensome efforts to sort things out.

Exploring the different objects in the attic characterizes the search going on within myself. Each object in the attic represents a different aspect of my life. The leather bound books with the gold borders and ownerless bookplates represent my educational goals. The beautiful ivory dress (once white, yellowed with age) that still sparkles is symbolic of my marriage. Trying on the turn-of-the-century, white, plumed hat (lady-in-waiting) is trying on the role of mother.

Another significant aspect of the Mirror Image, which keys into the struggle to determine my identity, is the unclear pattern or design of the tapestry. The beautiful, large tapestry of blue, green and yellow, with its unclear pattern, is how I see myself—not complete.

Several other features image myself as I would like to be. The beautiful stained-glass window with the bluish light cast by it depicts the way I would like my life to be: more character, more tradition, more quality, more diversity, more depth. The warm, balmy, summer day, which pours in through the window, depicts my ideal life. The arc light created by the opening of the window depicts knowledge and hope.

The one most significant point in the Mirror Image, which depicts my feelings towards my mother and the effect she has on me, comes at the point where the attic suddenly becomes dark. Although the window is open and it is sunny outside, no sunlight shines in the room. The one, naked light bulb dangling from the ceiling, which casts a dismal light, is symbolic of my mother's dismal outlook on life and the disenchanting effect it has on me. Finding the light switch and turning it to the on position does nothing to illuminate the room (my mind—my life), but in fact makes it even more dismal. The "on" position is my attempt to establish the mother-daughter relationship I never had.

The chronological order of the writings in my journal is significant in that it depicts the progression my mind made in presenting images, which brought to the surface feelings that I have been suppressing all my life.

Almost the very next writing in my journal, after the Mirror Image, deals directly with my struggle to find a family. In this writing I attempt to evaluate why I gave up my career to have a family. I list all the good reasons for having given up my job. The pressures, the anxieties, the sacrifices. I emphasize the impersonal practices of the big corporation. I try to convince myself I've done the right thing. Yet I write about how much I miss working, the people, the challenge. How, even after M was born, I would wander aimlessly around the house not really knowing what to do with myself. I was confused about my feelings. It isn't until much later in the journal, after a number of dreams in which the image of McDonald's presents itself time after time, that I realize that what I am feeling is the loss of and need for a family. I never went back to visit after I quit because it was too painful. McDonald's had been my family for almost ten years. Family is McDonald's whole philosophy. They market the family image to sell their product. Their employees are indoctrinated with the concept that they are "one big happy family."

Six of the eight dreams in my journal contained images of the people I worked with at McDonald's. Each of the dreams starts out the same way with me either working with the people or going to see them. However, the most significant dream with regards to giving up my McDonald's family was the one where I dreamt that I was in a basement doing worksheets on a long, narrow table. The room itself was long and narrow. In the dream I walked into my boss's office and saw my blue living room couch. When I went back to the table in the basement the work papers were gone and in their place were blue and pink baby clothes. When I went back to the office, the couch was gone. I asked my boss what had happened to the blue couch. He said he had sold it. I got upset and said that it was my couch and I'd never be able to replace it.

The basement in this dream, and as it appeared in other dreams, symbolizes the feelings I've been hiding or suppressing underneath. The long and narrow table and room depict how I had narrowed my life to MacDonald's. The blue living room couch appearing in the office symbolizes that I lived for my job. All my living was connected with MacDonald's. The work papers represent my MacDonald's family, which was replaced by the blue and pink baby clothes, which represents M. When I discovered my couch was gone from the office I was upset because my life was no longer connected with my McDonald's family and I knew I would never be able to replace it.

Feeling the loss of my McDonald's family is symbolized by my frequent

76

reference to death in the journal. In a writing on death and dying, which almost immediately follows my career writing, I write that I frequently found myself thinking about death in general. Furthermore, every time I got a newspaper I would read the obituaries first.

The next two writings in the journal deal with my struggle to find my family. In the first writing I wonder whether I've done the right thing in giving up my career, my MacDonald's family. The second writing deals with family and tradition on my husband's side.

Suddenly, some very strong feelings about my mother start to surface. In a writing of an imagined room I'm in the living room of the home I lived in as a child up to the age of thirteen. Feelings from my childhood start to surface. Feelings that I've successfully suppressed for twenty years. Feelings that I have convinced myself didn't exist. The emptiness of a house where four people live but no family life exists. No communication. No sharing. No caring. A mother who works to get away from a life she hates. A father who shows no feelings—no emotion. Never has anything to say. A brother who bums around and gets in trouble with the police.

I relive the feelings of hate and guilt. See again the just and confused look on my father's face. I wrote:

My mother and I leave the house, spend the night at my cousin's, and the next morning leave on a three-month camping trip through twenty-two states with my mother's friend and four kids. It is many days later and hundreds of miles later before I realize what has happened. I realize I can't even remember where we have been the first four days of the trip. I'm sitting in the back of a Ford station wagon watching endless miles of highway wind away like an endless ribbon unraveling and then suddenly disappearing. I'm thinking this isn't happening to me. I feel numb.

The next six pages of my journal reveal numerous accounts of my childhood and my relationship with my mother. At one point I wrote:

My mother ruled my brother and I with an iron hand. When we misbehaved she would whip us on the bare derriere with one of my father's leather belts. If she couldn't get hold of the belt quickly enough she used her high heel. If we called anyone names she'd wash our mouths out with soap. I feared my mother more than I disliked her. It seemed she was always angry.

I remember one time she was putting some dishes away in the buffet and she started crying. My first instinct was to put my arms around her and comfort her. I felt awkward so I just asked her why she was crying. She said she missed her mother.

Later on in the journal I wrote about a child dying of leukemia. This writing surfaced my mother's lack of affection; I could never remember her showing me

77

any affection as a child. My inner child had died of leukemia. Even now I can't stand touching or being touched by her. It makes me feel uncomfortable, unnatural. Makes my skin crawl.

The next writing in the journal further supports the theme of determining my identity and finding my family. I write about my brother-in-law's wife, C., my disappointment that she has rejected my efforts to befriend her. Now I realize that I wanted to be close to her because she would be more like a sister than just a friend. We had a common ground. I always wished I had a sister.

My mother's drinking is touched upon in the next writing. At this point I don't label it as a problem but lightly term it as "frequently getting sauced." As the writing progresses I try to establish evidence for the existence of a mother-daughter relationship. By the end of the writing, however, it becomes clear that it's contrived. And it is evident that I am confused about my identity, and about how I relate to other people and to life in general. I write: "I'm not sure of what I know or feel, or that what I think is important."

All the writings up to this point are collectively summarized in a dream about meeting three of my friends for lunch downtown. This dream is significant because it presented images, which depicted the dilemma I was in about the mother-daughter relationship I wanted and my desire for a sister. In this dream I was supposed to meet M, a friend, G, my ex-sister in law, and L, my sister-in-law. I was on lower Wacker Drive, the underground subway, running after the three girls. There were a maze of tunnels and halls. When I tried to cross the street to catch up with them, the oncoming traffic prevented me. Finally, I found a small, dismal teashop with yellow enamel walls. An old black Singer sewing machine sat in the lobby. The receptionist said she hadn't seen the girls, but I could overhear them talking. I couldn't make out what they were saying, but I didn't want to go in and sit down.

The underground and the maze of halls depict the confusion I'm in, the feelings I've been suppressing. The oncoming traffic I feel is my feelings. The old, black sewing machine is my mother. She makes the tearoom dismal. The yellow, enamel walls depict that I am beginning to become aware of my true feelings. I can't make out what the girls are saying and I don't want to go in and sit down with them because I really don't want to face up to the truth.

Then something happens which gives my mind the opportunity to present images depicting feelings of discontent, loneliness, disgust, and anger for a lifetime of obnoxious and abusive behavior from my mother. She comes to my house for Easter dinner with my in-laws and cousins. By 1:30 p.m. she is totally bombed. She embarrasses me and my father by insulting us and just by being her usual, obnoxious and overbearing drinking self. The day drags on and by 9:00 p.m. That night, after everyone has left, she starts in on me again. I lose control and start yelling and crying. Soon both my husband and my father are involved. She gets defensive and storms out.

78

This proves to be a turning point. I realize that what I had written earlier about her changing, since M was born, is untrue. I realize that in the past two years she has pulled at least three similar stunts. Finally, the dismal effect she has on me starts pouring out. I wrote:

My mother really depresses me. If I feel even a bit down, she'll bring me all the way down. It's her attitude; she discounts and over-simplifies everything in life. She never wants to go out of her way for anyone—make any effort. I hate to go to her house. Now that I think about it, I get depressed. I'm so mixed up. I feel like there's all this crap—stuff packed in my head—deep down—all jumbled up—and I can't get it out. Can't get it sorted out. I don't know if I want to. I'm tired of thinking about it. Tired of wondering what's nagging me at the back of my mind.

Suddenly the floodgates open and a deluge of imaginations and dreams occur. My mind takes the opportunity to release images representing years and years of suppressed feelings. One of the most significant of these writings (and of any writing in my journal) deals with the loneliness I experienced during a good part of my life. The loneliness of not having a family. The loneliness of having a mother who finds her companionship in a bottle of booze. It is almost one year since my parents have separated. I have been living alone with my mother in an apartment in a strange city. I wrote:

I'm alone as always. My mother is working as she does every Sunday and Saturday. It will be four or five hours before she comes home. When she does she will have her bottle of booze to keep her company. She will be tired—in a bad mood. She will sit and drink and read magazines or sew or something until she goes to bed or passes out. Maybe this will be a night she will go out boozing with her friends from work. She will come waltzing in at eleven or twelve at night—three sheets to the wind, reeking of garlic, booze and nicotine. And she will sit and read her magazines or sew, or whatever, and drink some more.

My journal entry continues, recounting the day following. As I wake the next morning, Easter morning, to the sounds of families returning from church, I am empty. Lonely. I'm not alive—just existing. In attempts to fill a huge void in my life—to salvage the day—I hit the local hangouts to try and find just one person to talk to. The usual hangout, the bowling alley proves to be unfruitful. I wrote:

Easter Sunday, everyone will be with their families. Together. Having dinner at home, or going out to some relative's or friend's home to be together. But not me.

My last hope is Bert's grille. I run almost six of the ten blocks before slowing down to a normal pace. Nonchalantly I stroll up to the front of the small restaurant, pull on the handle of the front door only to find it won't open. Bert's is closed. Empty. Void. I peer into the front window, nose against the glass, my hand shadowing my eyes. Straight ahead I see myself in the mirrors behind the counter. The expressionless face now wears the look of despair. I feel empty. Numb. I stand against the window for some time, eyes closed, just letting the tears flow.

After a while I pull myself together and slowly walk back to the apartment. I feel like I'm watching a movie with the sound turned off. I can't even feel the wind blowing through my hair or the hot sun beating down on my face. Everything looks dingy and dismal even though it's sunny.

This writing upset me so much that half way through I had to put it aside, go into another room and cry. As I was writing, years and years of days like this one came flashing back to me. The devastating feeling of loneliness and despair came back so strong it was if this Easter of almost twenty years ago had just happened yesterday. Twenty years ago I didn't cry these tears. I was too numb. Too used to feeling and being alone, even in a crowd.

At this point I finally realized that she was the dismal effect in all my dreams and imaginations. I realized that I had spent many years feeling guilty and unhappy. Unhappy because I was lonely and wanted a family life. Guilty because my mother hated her life—had wanted to leave my father, but had stayed with him because of my brother and I. She blamed us for her unhappiness. When she finally did leave my father, when I was thirteen, she was stuck with me. A burden.

I had sorted a ton of things out. I knew we'd never have the mother-daughter relationship I had hoped for. I also knew there was no turning back. I had crossed a huge bridge and she was not on the other side. Now that I was aware of my conflicts in finding a family, one to replace my MacDonald's, and one to replace the one I never had, my mind grasped the opportunity to present images of the long journey I had taken. This is the most significant dream because the images collectively symbolize my entire struggle.

I dreamt I went on a trip with two friends. We each had our own cars. We were traveling a long time, going south through mountains and green forests. I was driving a white Volkswagen and my two friends drove luxury cars. I kept having car trouble and would have to stop periodically to fix my car. I was afraid they would leave me behind and I'd get lost. I didn't know where I was. I was completely unfamiliar with the surroundings.

This part of the dream clearly keys into the struggle I had been going through. The two friends were me, the child and finally the adult, who zipped along through life oblivious to what was happening with my feelings. The white Volkswagen depicts that I, myself, was down to basics, aware—no more luxury cars just skimming along. The car trouble represents having to get hold of my feelings

80

periodically. I was frightened of getting lost and maybe not getting things sorted out.

At one point in the dream I stop at a car wash; all of a sudden bubbles poured out of the hood. They just kept coming and coming. I was afraid my friends would get upset and leave me behind—but I remained calm and tried to correct the situation.

This part about the bubbles pouring from the hood of the car represents the outpour of my feelings that I had suppressed for so many years. It was alarming and I was afraid of the awareness that was coming over me. I was afraid that I would change and I didn't know if I could handle it, if it would be for the best.

As the dream progressed I realized that I knew a lot of people in the line of cars at the car wash; I was no longer afraid of my friends leaving me behind.

Finally my car was washed and I wiped it dry with a red sham. It was a beautiful, sunny day. I was standing under a beautiful, huge, green tree.

The last part of the dream symbolizes my realization that I had no reason to fear the feelings that had been uncovered. That it was okay to let go of that child and adult zipping along in their luxury cars, now that my Volkswagen was washed clean of all the bad feelings. The sunny day represented my awareness, the beautiful, green tree, the growth I have made.

I know now some of the significant experiences in my life and how they have affected me. And I also know that there's still a lot to sort out. I don't know if my mother and I will ever talk again. I do know it will never be as it was before Easter. Too much has happened over the years. I've grown—before I was operating in a vacuum.

The floodgates are open and everything is pouring in. The attic from the Mirror Image is coming back now. It's bright and sunny. Fresh air is blowing in from the window. The cobwebs are almost entirely gone now. The only dust that remains is a few smudges here and there. All the boxes are stacked in neat rows ready to be looked into. The light switch has a piece of tape over it with a note that read, "No longer in use!"

The disenchantment and dismalness that appeared in the attic and many of my other writings is my mother and her dismal outlook on life—the effect that it has had on me. The significance of the image of the light switch is that I have the power to control the situation. I can turn it off or on. She can't. I have chosen to secure it in the off position—but note, only by use of tape. Apparently, at this point my intentions are not permanent. Maybe once I completely sort through the many boxes and trunks, I'll decide.

That dismal light was distorting my vision—my perspective on life. At least now without her around to disenchant me . . . me.

J.

She combs her journal, entry by entry, giving herself a narrative of meaning as it unfolds. The journal sequence itself is her structure.

The essay has a fine, beginning-ending shape. She brings back the prime image with which she introduced the essay—but with a difference. With her mind cleaning, the attic has changed.

Several times as she interprets her images she simply makes life identifications, with the word "depicts": The red ribbon depicts her passionate self; the dismal, attic light depicts her mother's influence. Meaning is implied, sometimes clearly, in these life identifications; but it might be stated more clearly *as it applies to her life.* Leaving life identifications as such may (or may not) make the point, since the point is *implied*, not stated.

Suggested Writing:

You might try a working essay of your journal, perhaps a section that stands out as most important. Explore what seems your most significant image, and the images in its neighborhood. Or you might start with a sequence of images that appears to be on the same subject. Follow your instincts.

6 ESSAY/MEMOIR

Memory is the great organizer of human consciousness.　　　*Susanne Langer,*
philosopher

The essay allows you to ramble in a way that reflects the mind at work. . . . the track
of a person's thoughts struggling to achieve some understanding of a problem is the
plot, is the adventure.

Phillip Lopate

The essay makes visible the patterns of an individual's thoughts. It allows us to see
the process of contemplation that results in understanding that in turn leads to
action.

Pamela Klass Mittlefehldt

Every essay is the only one of its kind.　　　*Lydia Fakundiny*

Follow the accident; fear the fixed plan—that is the rule.　　　*John Fowles, novelest*

Essay. Nearly 500 years ago the Frenchman, Michel de Montaigne, introduced
the world to the "essay," more a way of writing than a form. It is an invitation to
the mind to do in writing what it does on its own, always: to explore experience,
using whatever resources it can find, and taking what path it will.

The essay is also called the "personal essay" these days; but it is just as
commonly called "essay," so that's the term I'll use. A major form within essay,
especially these days, is "memoir." Memoir, of course, suggests memories as a
major component; significant, usually extended, memories (narratives, stories) are
essential to the "memoir," not always to the essay. Memoirs anchor themselves to
one or more significant memories.

Sometimes memoir just narrates the memory, tells the story with little or no
comment. Sometimes a character within the story comments on its meaning. And
sometimes the author will explore its meaning outside the story.

"Memoir" was formerly used as a term for public figures' written memories of
important happenings within their times, usually book length. These days, memoir
is used for the writings of all sorts of persons remembering what was important to
their lives. Current memoirs range in length from short pieces to book length.

Though memoir no longer concerns only important public figures and events, it still tends (but not always) to be a little more public, more world-connected, than personal essay (or autobiography).

You've probably got several significant memories written in your journal, so you've got the material for a memoir. And perhaps by now you've worked a *theme* developing within your journal, so you've got the material for an essay and some awareness of meaning.

But what is a "theme?" In a musical piece, a song for instance, a theme is the melody, a pattern of notes repeated in its verses. In other musical pieces the theme may go through variations—but is always recognizable: that succession of notes conveying a particular course of feeling, with a particular tone quality, rhythm, and key. A melody is so distinctive that it only takes hearing a few notes to be identified. Theme defines a piece of music.

Theme also defines essay/memoir: an "idea" runs through the piece like a melody. That idea is worked with, like variations on a musical piece.

You've seen this in several writings: "The Little Green House on the Corner," the entry concerning an uncle's death from cancer, the Girl Scout entry, "Bobby," the bar scene, and a sister's sketch of her brother. In each a particular idea, emotion, and attitude is worked with and given a particular form, like a melody.

Memoir: Does one memory (or image of any sort) stand out? Does it "picture" what you've been discovering? Begin with that, just telling the memory, or describing the image (whether actual or imagined). Does the memory *extend* itself, or draw in other memories? Keep on with it. Does it convey its theme with little or no explanation? Then *don't explain (or explain little); let the narrative suggest the idea.* Just tell the story until it feels complete.

Does a character begin to explain meanings within the story? Does that feel right? Fine. Let the character explain.

Do you feel the impulse, as narrator or author, to explain the meaning of the events unfolding? Watch that impulse to explain. Does the story *present* its theme strongly? Then let it; your explanation may weaken the theme.

But perhaps some explanation will make the meaning clearer, stronger. Fine. Trust your instincts.

Do you want to talk about the writing process as you go? Fine. That's typical of memoirs and essays.

Essay: Do you have a theme clearly in mind, one that you can *state*? Do you feel like explaining your theme at the start? Or would an image best present your theme, leaving explanations until later? Start with an explanation or an image, whichever feels right. But again, watch the tendency to explain.

What image comes next to mind in connection with the first image or explanation? How much explanation does the image need to connect with the first image or explanation? How does it develop your theme?

84

What image comes next to mind?

Again, talk about the writing process if you feel like it.

These are just a few suggestions as to how you might get started with memoir and essay. You may have your own ideas as to form, which don't follow these patterns at all. Fine. Memoir and essay are flexible ways of writing oriented to the experience and thought of just one author–you.

Keep one thing in mind always: your theme, your melody. That will hold the piece together. But if another theme intrudes, respect it. Then take one of two options: 1) If the second theme feels like *the* theme–abandon the first; 2) but if the second theme is a variation on the first theme, connected to it, then make the connection, and pursue the variation, as musical pieces do.

As Fowles writes in the epigraph: "Follow the accident; fear the fixed plan . . ."

Most of the essays/memoirs you are about to read make use of narrative or story, usually in the form of a memory. Since the beginning of history, stories have given us our most complete understanding of what it is to live as humans. We like stories, we like to listen to them, and to tell them. They draw us in; we believe them.

Does your story have to be historical, true to fact? Generally, but not necessarily. Can you have persons say what you *thought* they said or what they *might* have said? Yes. Can you invent a scene that *might* have happened, or *should* have happened? Sure. You may already have the scene you need in an imagination written in your journal. Invent, as long as your invention feels true to your experience. Your mind is always "inventing" the truth of your experience. That's what the essay has to discover and share.

The following memoir concerns a death two years past in a Mexican village.

It's always the same; it's like a dream. It's like I left a piece of me there and I keep going back. Any time, any place, when I'm happy, when I'm sad--out of nowhere just, BAM. There I am again. It's sunrise, maybe about six, and the sun is almost blinding. Which is really weird because he died at one in the morning, in the middle of the night. Anyway, it's sunrise. I'm at the bottom of the steep road that leads to the front of his house. The street is made of cobblestone; I hate these stupid rocks. I'm running. So heavy. So tired. Gotta go faster. My chest is heaving and the world starts to spin and I gotta keep running. Finally I'm at the doors.

The doors are green and white and they swing open to the sides. They're so heavy. Get in, stupid. Kick it. The doors finally swing open and there is a crowd in the living room, all people he has helped, no doubt. This room is my sanctuary. I am surrounded by my roots. The pictures of our past hang on the walls.

(God this is hard; I've never spoken to anyone about this. I've kept it inside for two long years. You would think this would be easier after such a long time.)

I'm standing in the middle of the room; the doors are directly in front of me. He is lying on the bed to my right. But I can't go there right now; I can't even make myself turn that way. There is a seven-foot dresser to my left. I can see their reflection in the mirror. I can see them gathered around the bed. And his breathing, it's like a cold scream that cuts through me and sends shivers down my back. It fills the room and drowns out all the crying. I can't do this now. I keep turning to my left and there is the doorway to the kitchen. It's only about five and a half feet tall so I have to duck to get through.

I'm in the kitchen now but I can still hear his breathing. Why doesn't he just go? What is he fighting for? The kitchen is as beautiful as I remember it. The wood stove in the right hand corner of the room is about 60 years old. Directly across the room from it, in the left hand corner, is the gas stove. Next to the gas stove is the refrigerator, which still has the stickers I put there almost 20 years ago. A small table with four chairs fills the middle of the room. This place might as well be an oven; I can't stay here. But I can't go back into the living room. His breathing is driving me crazy. I have to see him.

Then I'm just there. At the foot of the bed. Why doesn't everyone just stop crying? He doesn't look that bad; except for his breathing he looks like he is sleeping. I wish his eyes would open, but they tell me they haven't opened for three days now. I loved the way his eyes looked at me, almost mocking me, because he had a better life than I could ever have. His laugh, so full of life. Even when he was angry he laughed. When he was sad he would sit and watch the sunset, and he would smile. The greatest man I've ever known now lying in a bed, dying. Why don't they all shut up! He is lying on his back, his arms at his sides. His skin, so soft and wrinkled; it's paper thin. And cold. The pain those hands have felt, the work they have done. Hands that once caressed and were caressed will soon lie in a dark cold grave. His chest rises and falls as his breathing turns to gagging and coughing.

"Can you hear me grandpa? It's me, Armandito. Do you know who I am?" I would like to believe that the opening of his eyes means that he remembers me, but I know that is not true. His eyes are roaming the room as if he were looking for something or someone. Then he looks at me and says, "Who will take care of the children? Will you take care of them?" There is great exhaustion in his eyes, and with tears in mine I answer, "Yes, I'll take care of them." After that he closes his eyes and with one last deep breath, he leaves us forever.

Till this day I wonder what I promised him. Shortly after his funeral I left that small town and I vowed never to return. My grandmother passed away a couple of months after that. But I couldn't go back there. She'll just have to forgive me. It's been over two years now and I haven't been able to forget. It used to scare me, but it doesn't anymore.

I wish I knew what I promised him. I'll just have to go back there and ask him. Some day.

Armando Jaquez Z.

86

This memoir is different from an essay that announces its subject. Suppose Armando had begun: "In this essay I am going to discuss . . ." You can imagine how that would have ruined his story. Even if he had begun: "My grandfather died at one in the morning, but that's not how I remember it," the memoir would have had a different character.

Instead he brings us along with him in imagination: "BAMM. There I am again. It's sunrise . . . I'm at the bottom of the steep road that leads to the front of his house." All we know is that it's the house of someone who is dying, and that Armando must get there soon. We don't need to know more. If he began to explain, his voice would go flat, the drama would disappear, and we might soon be bored: "My grandfather is on his deathbed with his entire family gathered around. This great man is dying in pain . . ."

Instead he takes us along to see, hear, and feel through his senses, and listen to his thoughts. That's the mark of a good memoir: to give us the look, the sound, and the feel of the experience (its taste and smell as well), moment by moment. And where appropriate, to share thoughts. But explanation shouldn't dominate; memory should.

Armando takes us immediately into the house: "Get in stupid. Kick it." Suddenly we're into a crowded living room with "all the people he has helped," Armando's "roots," pictures of his past hanging on the walls. He doesn't have to stop to explain to us that it's his grandfather dying. (We'll find out before long.) Just the few things he's said and shown to us imply the experience is charged with his history, so charged that he can't go in. And then, with one chilling metaphor, he brings us into the presence of immanent death: "And his breathing, it's like a cold scream that cuts through me and sends shivers down my back."

He can't take it, turns to the kitchen, and ducks through the low doorway. But that breathing follows him, and confronts him again when he re-enters the living room. Breath, nothing speaks to us so powerfully of life and death as breath ("the breath of life"). It's perfect, symbolically, for the entire experience; Armando returns to his grandfather's breathing again and again.

The kitchen—just from what he describes, we know that the family, and this man, are short of stature, live in rustic conditions, and that Armando's experience of the place goes way back. He wants to stay in the kitchen; the dying man's breathing is "driving [him] crazy." But suddenly—"I have to see him"—he's in the living room. We've gone through that struggle with him, moment by moment; and now, in the moments left before his grandfather dies, we will experience every question, wish, memory, and perception of the scene that goes through Armando's head, fractures of thought and perception included. It's believable, impacts us; he's not trying to *make* it good, to *make* it flow—or to explain. It's bad: "the greatest man [he's] ever known now lying in a bed dying." Like the experience itself, the writing doesn't flow smoothly:

Why don't they just shut up. He's lying on his back, his arms at his sides. His skin, so soft and wrinkled; it's paper thin. And cold. The pain those hands have felt, the work they have done.

And he can't explain: "Hands that once caressed and were caressed will soon lie in a dark cold grave." But he can, and does, give us the impact of these events just by relating (it seems) everything he's taking in, feeling, and thinking.

And then, as his grandfather's death approaches, speech comes into the picture. Armando doesn't give in to the all-too-common tendency to generalize: *My grandfather seemed to wake, and asked who would take care of the children, whether I would take care of the children. I told him that I would.* He doesn't generalize; he gives all the particulars, moment by moment.

His eyes are roaming the room as if he were looking for something or someone. Then he looks at me and says," Who will take care of the children? Will you take care of them?" There is great exhaustion in his eyes, and with tears in mine I answer, "Yes, I'll take care of them." After that he closes his eyes and with one last deep breath, he leaves us forever.

Finally, he questions what has really happened, the meaning of the promise, and voices the conflict that remains about returning to that scene, his roots. He could try to explain here at the end, come to a conclusion; he doesn't need to, and he can't. Instead, Armando presents a powerful sense of what death means, the death of a beloved grandfather back in the old country.

Memoirs aren't tied to explanation, nor to fact. Armando implies that he actually took the trip home. But he suggests right off that the visit is (also) imaginative, a memory recurring without warning, and not entirely accurate. His grandfather actually died in the middle of the night, not in the middle of the morning, as the memoir has it. In the memoir, the exact time of his grandfather's death is unimportant. The important thing is the *personal* reality of the experience, which may contrast with the bare facts. It is the reality-to-Armando that counts. His grandfather died sometime in the morning, the sun rising into the heavens. Symbolically that might make sense several ways.

The following memoir begins with the recollection of a single incident that occurred as the author left high school one afternoon. The incident affects him deeply; he can't get it out of his mind. He begins to think about its meaning. Before long another incident comes to mind, one never resolved. Realizations pour in, and before long a vexing puzzle is solved.

School's out for the day, time to go home and find something better to do. I hit the aluminum-framed door exactly at 3:05. The weather outside is miserable: cloudy, cold and slightly foggy from the falling mist. Spring is on its way; shortly I will be out of this school—for good! No longer will I have to walk home in weather like this.

The mist lightly comes down, but heavy enough to keep the pavement wet. I catch up with a friend of mine a few feet past the doors. We start reminiscing about the day's events, who got into a fight with who, and did ya hear about so and so doing this or that (the same old bullshit, just a different day).

We walk vigorously to get the school out of our sight. A kid catches my attention running at a jogger's pace towards the street to catch a ride or something. Slipping behind a car that just passed he looks down the street in the direction that traffic is pointing. Turning my head back in the direction I am walking, I see a brown, Delta 88 accelerating out of the center lane and into the fire lane attempting to gain some ground. The car clips the kid's right leg, knocking it out from underneath; he falls on the hood and smacks his head off the windshield--hard! I can't believe it; the driver just hit this kid.

She slams on the brake. The kid begins sliding down the hood; I think for sure the car will stop and he'll be thrown a few feet in front of the car. But that doesn't happen; the car keeps moving, sliding over the wet pavement. I watch the kid with what consciousness he possesses hang onto the front end. There is nothing to grasp. The car's surface is too wet for him to maintain a good grip. His legs are already under the car. I watch as a bad situation keeps getting worse. He loses his grip. He disappears. The car suddenly jumps.

I can't believe what I am witnessing. Why couldn't I get out of school sooner?

My pace has slowed as I unbelievingly watch this helpless kid being trampled, the automobile bouncing slightly as the chassis rolls over his body.

The world is quiet; I hear only the sounds of rubber screeching over the pavement and limbs thumping off the underside of floorboards. Something that should last a few seconds has turned into an eternity. The car jumps once more as the rear tire comes into contact. His body bounces out from underneath the car making a complete revolution in the air until it flops on the ground like a fish.

All this looks so fake, like he's a dummy. But it's not, this is for real; that is a human being.

There he lies, helpless, after going through what is for sure to be the death of him. He raises his left knee into the air; I turn, look straight ahead, and continue walking as if it never happened.

I am miserable for a week; I can't forget what happened. The accident plays over and over in my mind. Trying to sleep at night is difficult. My stomach remains cramped and upset from the disgusting sounds his body made off the car. I keep asking myself, why didn't I stay, why did I keep walking like some heartless savage? I told myself I wanted no part of being an eye witness; I didn't want a police report made of what I saw happen; this could lead to testifying in court. I just wanted to put this all in the past. Walking away was the best solution.

The emotional impact subsided in a couple of weeks, but something persisted in my mind. Each time I heard cars skidding in the distance or new reports of fatal car accidents I would instantly flash back to that miserable day.

I accept the fact that people are being struck by cars every minute of the day and that it is an ugly fact of life that will always exist. But for years my conscience haunted me. The accident affected me more than I believed it to. I couldn't help but think that walking away to avoid any further involvement was the only thing that bothered me. And for years the question of "what" remained unanswered, until a few days ago when it came to me while taking a shower.

I recall the endless number of nights when I lay awake imagining, hypothesizing, how Richard was killed by the train. I attempted to picture--just what was the accident that resulted in such a deadly outcome. For hours I envisioned him being struck: the reaction on his face moments before life was to be knocked out of his body, the sounds the impact made, his body falling to one side of the tracks or worse yet, flying through the air until it found a final resting place. I was curious, looking for answers that made ends meet; why him, why was my brother taken away from me so cruelly? I had a hard time believing that the laws of nature, the laws of physics, allowed something like this to happen.

There was no place to draw any answers from. I was only eight years old. I knew very little of the cruelties the world possesses. I was a kid, there was no reason for me to be concerned. Even as I grew older the fact remained that I could only guess about the events that led to Richard's death. My family and my friends tried telling me, but their words held very little meaning. To me, "seeing is believing." Seeing that kid get hit by the car proved to me that this world is very cruel.

I kept walking because the questions I had about Richard's death were subconsciously answered. Of course this wasn't a person being struck by a train, but the connection gave me enough information, and I didn't like what I discovered. To this day I realize this must be true about my conclusions. Why else would seeing that kid being hit have depressed me so much? I didn't know him, and he wasn't a friend of mine or a member of my family. What he was, was an unfortunate person that was killed in the same, ugly way as Richard. That put to rest questions that have been circling my mind for years. To the kid, the car's impact was his destiny; to me the car's deadly impact meant that I could move on. My many curiosities about Richard's death are no longer with me. The reality of the car accident provided me with the momentum to leave Richard's accident in the past, and remember him for the time he was on this earth, remember him as my brother.

Although I no longer lie awake at night putting the pieces together about Richard's death, I do, however, wonder just how valid my life is. (I can't help but think this after experiencing these two tragedies.) I am young, yet with a full life ahead to live. But so was Richard, even that kid. It scares me to death knowing that tomorrow I could be gone, that I could screw up and put myself in a situation that would determine the validity of my continuing existence, that I could put my *family back in the same situation as it was eleven years ago. Right now as I sit at this desk I can recall the endless number of times I have put my ass on the line and am lucky enough to be here today to put this essay together.*

I can look back and remind myself that life is too damn precious not to make it count. I realize now that the things that provided me with a rush in the past were incredibly stupid and could have put me in the same place as Richard.

B. D.

This piece begins with even less explanation than Armando's, in fact, none. Without introduction the writer brings us into that cold, rainy afternoon with all of its ugly particulars, so detailed that we are watching the "trampling" in slow motion.

> *The world is quiet; I hear only the sounds of rubber screeching over the pavement and limbs thumping off the underside of floor boards. Something that should last a few seconds has turned into an eternity. The car jumps once more as the rear tire comes into contact. His body bounces out from underneath the car making a complete revolution in the air until it flops on the ground like a fish.*

The description works, in all of its gruesomeness, which is absolutely necessary. It is through the description told in just these ugly particulars that his meaning will emerge. Descriptions, as you've seen many times over, carry information, meaning, messages. Shorten the description and you may not only shorten the message, but abort it.

Of course he doesn't want the message to emerge just yet: "I turn, look straight ahead, and continue walking as if it never happened." But he's "miserable for a week;" he "can't forget what happened." Meaning is emerging. He gives us the story of that emergence.

At first it's little more than rationalizations as to why he didn't stay and offer himself as an eye witness. But his mind is intent on solving the old problem of his brother's death. His mind persists, presents him with images of other accidents that bring him back to the memory of that afternoon. He continues to rationalize the incident, but his mind won't let it go: "what" remains unanswered; what was this about, really?

Just recently, though he doesn't mention it, he's been writing in his journal, not only recounting the accident (of years before) but also discussing the early loss of his brother and its effect upon the family. It's not surprising, then, that the "what" question gets answered, even there in the shower. In the journal his mind has taken the opportunity to get him focused on the matter and thinking about it. As essays often do, he spells out that process. He's spent endless nights awake "hypothesizing how Richard was killed by the train," trying to picture his death. But, he writes, "There was no place to draw any answers from."

It took just one vivid event ("seeing is believing," he writes) to answer his question–but it took describing that event and thinking about it to bring those answers to awareness: "Seeing that kid get hit by the car proved to me that this world is very cruel." The kid was "an unfortunate person that was killed in the same, ugly way as Richard." He's got his answer to "what;" now he can put it all "to rest."

Then he extends his thinking, brings it home to his own life. If the world can be this cruel at any moment, he realizes that he could, and has, put his own life at risk. Life, he concludes, "is too damn precious not to make it count."

The following piece falls within the more classic definition of "memoir," though the event remembered is only an evening long. This memoir reminds us of the world of junior high school, nearly any junior high in the USA. This "world" is captured within the particulars of the author's experience.

STAIRWAY TO HEAVEN

Junior high is the best. I belong to this club, "The Boyfriend of the Week Club." I think my friends and I switch boyfriends more than we get dropped off at the mall. Which is twice a week.

It's Friday, the best day of the week, 3:00; my mom just got home from work. I grab her purse, "Come on mom it's Friday. I have to get something new to wear tonight." She tells me I better take my babysitting money. "I have $30," I say, knowing that she'll pay for half once we are there.

Once we're there I see about twenty people I know. My mom vows never to come shopping with me again because I stop every two feet to talk to someone. What am I supposed to do, act like I don't see my friends? I pick out a cute little shirt. My mom complains that I have ten others exactly like it. (Which I do.) When we get up to the counter and find out that the shirt's on sale my mom says, "Keep your money, you spoiled kid." Then we drive home listening to my music, which my mom says is her music. I can't see my mom at a Grateful Dead show, or Zeppelin, or Floyd. I of course tell my mommy how great she is, and thank her a billion times for the shirt, so she's not too mad on Sunday when I give her my progress report.

As soon as we get home my little sister reads me off a list of people who called while I was gone. Before she gets half-way done the phone rings. It's one of my 10 closest, bestest friends, Christina. I ask her what she's wearing, tell her about my new shirt and we decide whose parents are driving and whose are picking up. My mom says she'll drive. Christina says hers will pick up.

My next-door neighbor, Mary, one of my 10 closest, bestest friends, comes over. (Her parents never drive 'cause they are like 80.) She says she has nothing to wear. Which is a huge crisis at our age. (She does this every week. I don't mind 'cause they have a lot of kids in her family and they can't afford that much.) So, I

92

let her go shopping in "Meash's Closet." After we are dressed I do my hair and hers. Then we each stuff as much of her older sister's makeup as we can in our pockets. (Our parents say we're too young.)

It's 6:30, time to go. The dance starts at 7:00. My mom mumbles something about class and women and fashionably late. Christina, Mary, and I are too busy belting out the lyrics to "Sugar Magnolia" to hear her. We don't understand this fashionably late stuff. We always have to be at the dance 20 minutes early, everyone does. We don't care if we have to freeze our butts off waiting for them to open the door. It is the cool thing to do.

We get out of the car the way the movie stars get out of the limo's on awards night. All eyes on us. We smile and say "Hi!" to all the people we could give a shit about. Our half-dressed little bodies are freezing. Finally, they open the doors. We pay our fives and run to the bathroom to put on our faces. Then we run back upstairs to the gym where the dance is, with our over-applied, stolen makeup on.

Girls on the right, boys on the left. We all, the girls, start dancing, but making sure not to cross the dreaded middle of the gym to the boys' side. We try to be as seductive as possible (well as seductive as MTV and Madonna has taught our little 12 & 13-year old bodies how to be.) Basically we know the boys are watching. We laugh, overly loud, so the guys think we are talking about them, which we are. We are calling dibs on the boys we love.

Then one of my other 10 closest, bestest friends, Sarah, says she is going to go ask Jeff to dance the last slow song with me. My closest, bestest friends all hold me back as I say no. Sarah runs across the dance floor, into enemy territory, and asks the hottest boy in the whole world (on that Friday) to dance with me. Which is exactly what I wanted her to do. I can't look, too afraid that he is laughing or shaking his head, No. Christina, Mary, Kelly and Shannon (my closest, bestest friends) do, though. They tell me he nodded yes and his friends slapped him five. Thank God! I mean that would really suck if he said no, seeing that I already have our whole life planned out.

We are going to get married, live in a white house with a porch all around it and a white picket fence, a tree with a tire swing, two children, a boy and a girl. Oh yeah, the kids will be twins. Did I mention he's a doctor? That story never changes, just my husband. Well, enough about our future.

The DJ says, "Let's slow things down for the last time with a little, Led Zeppelin." Every week it's the same last song, "Stairway to Heaven." Which didn't bother anyone seeing that it was the longest song we ever heard. Not to mention it was every couples' song in the whole junior high.

He struts across the dance floor towards me kind of the way that Danny Zucco, John Travolta, struts towards Sandy, Olivia Newton John, in Grease. I can feel myself getting extremely hot and red in the face. I turn to my closest, bestest friends, "Do I look OK? Is my (over-applied-in-the-bathroom, obnoxiously red) lipstick OK?" I get reassured as he approaches. He nods his head so ultra coolly towards the dance floor, like Dillon Mcay, Luke Perry, from 90210 would do. He brings me onto the dance floor by my hand. I feel so secure and happy and I'm just going to pop! His hand is so sweaty—I swear I will never wash my hand again. Oh God, his best friend, Adam, the second coolest boy in the school, just asked Christina to dance. How cool is this?!? We are set. She mouths, "Oh my God," to me. I mouth back, "I know," and we both mouth the loudest in-our-head screams that only we can hear.

By the end of the song are bodies are so close. We both have our heads comfortably on their sweaty, hormone stricken bodies. Then they kiss us. Christina and I are both totally grossed out, but would never let on. We can't understand why anyone would want to stick his or her tongue in anyone else's mouth. Yuck.

That's it, this week's dance is over. I'm on cloud 9. We all pile into Christina's mom's truck after sneaking one last secret kiss. After a while we finally convince Christina's mom into letting her sleep over. (She was still pretty mad at us about the sneaking of the makeup thing.)

We stay up all night watching scary movies, planning our weddings and how our children are going to play together. At about 3:00 my dad comes in and he's not too happy. We were supposed to be in bed by 1:00. We are being a little loud I guess. Isn't that what teenage girls are supposed to do. OOPS. Oh, well he's still going to make us the best pancakes in the world in the morning.

Then Monday in school I make sure I look extra good for my future hubby. I look for the love of my life everywhere. He's holding hands with one of my so-called closest, bestest friends, Kelly. Oh, I hate her. I guess they went skating on Saturday and he told her we broke up and he asked her out. How could she do this to me? I will never talk to her again--'till about lunchtime. See, I just had English with his best friend, Adam; he's my new love. You know, the one that Christina danced with Friday.

Michelle Desmarais

With the brains and voice of a junior high girl, but with the awareness of her adult self, Michelle brings us into the world of junior high school without ever going outside her story to explain its theme. But her theme is perfectly transparent: this is what junior high feels like, looks like, and sounds like. Junior high is a friendly tribe, free-floating romance, hormones in orbit, and the imitation of movie stars, Led Zeppelin, MTV, and Madonna, all of it simply shown.

You can't miss the several devices of voice Michelle uses to give her memoir its particular character, its unique melody.

The following essay details the experience of a woman working on an Alzheimer's unit in a home for veterans–and the changes that occurred when new management took over.

I work in an Alzheimer/wanderers unit. All of the men who live with us are veterans. To be eligible to make this home, they must have served our country

94

during wartime. They come from all walks of life. Alzheimer disease plays no favorites. Some were bankers, others lithographers, mechanics and builders. The varied list goes on and on. When the unit was being planned five years ago, the staff was to be hand picked. You needed to apply and be interviewed for the positions. A head nurse was carefully chosen. Training was required. There was a ten-part instructional video series that was a requirement to acceptance. Numerous in-services were held to train us in techniques for successful interaction with this population. The importance of interaction, activity, and mental stimulation were especially stressed. (We even were to have our own trained activity person.) Special classes in diverting and disarming aggressive behavior were held. We had to learn to "just walk away and try again later, keep your cool at all times." Not an easy thing to do when someone is punching and kicking you or slapping you across the face or pulling your hair. There were feeding techniques to learn. We were required to be certified in CPR.

Although most of us had been working in geriatrics for a long time and had dealt with these issues on a daily basis, this was going to be a unit of just wandering dementia and Alzheimer patients living together in one, large space. This is a horse of an entirely different color, as we were about to find out. We were ready, willing, and, hopefully, able to meet the new frontier.

Finally, the space was complete, and the staff had been chosen, hand picked right down to the porter who cleaned the floors. We had carte blanche. Anything that we asked for; special foods, plants, things for activities, decorative shelving to keep things in view but out of reach for curious hands came upon request. It was a wide-open space. Plenty of room to wander.

The area had formerly been the dormitory, housing forty-four veterans. Each sleeping area had held six to eight beds per room. The residents had eaten their meals in the main dining room located in the adjoining building. In our new space, four veterans now shared a room. We had our own dining room. Meals were served using a table at the bedside. An oval table to seat the gentlemen who needed some assistance occupied the center of the room. This room was also to be used for social gatherings and activities. An attractive border ran halfway down the walls in the hallways all through the unit as a guide as to which way to go. It was even carried across the entrance door so that the space seemed unbroken and drew attention away from and disguised the exit door. The soft blue, soothing-to-the-eye, drapes on the windows slid rather than having a pull chord that might get tangled around a neck. The guys could easily open them by themselves. A rail was placed across the very large window so that the vets would be aware that they could not just walk through, that it was not an open space.

Alzheimer's is one of medicines biggest mysteries. It affects over four million Americans—one in every ten of those over sixty-five; nearly half of those are eighty-five and older. And the toll is rising as people live longer. It is truly devastating and less treatable than almost any other disease. Despite twenty years of research, no one knows how the brain-killing disease arises, never mind how to cure it.

95

All of the residents on our unit are men, ranging in age from as young as sixty-eight (our youngest was forty-nine) to some who are over ninety years old. They have people who love them. Often they don't recognize their loved ones when they come to visit.

One man was a bank president. He has been with us for two years. He asks on an average of thirty times a day, "Where am I? Where's my car? Where's my room, I want to lie down." He can carry on a conversation that makes sense most days. He still has his sense of humor on a good day. He is always a gentleman. Some things don't change. Recently, he fell and broke a hip. While he was in the hospital, we had to pack his things to go to another unit. Our unit is only for people who wander and are not safe to in an unsupervised environment. Among his things we found a pad with several pages of correspondence to his family. The words brought tears to our eyes. July 10: "Please bring shorts for summer. Have you made arrangements for me to come home? I await your reply." July 29: "Thank you for the shorts. I can be ready on a moments notice. When can you pick me up to go home?" August 15: "Please make arrangements for me to come home soon. I want to live a normal life." He then signed his full name and what he thought were his address and phone number. He's one of the lucky ones at this point of the disease, believe it or not. In six months or a year, he might not know his name, never mind if he even has a family.

Another was a lithographer. He is sixty-eight years old, a virile, handsome man with a great sense of humor, six children who don't come to see him, and no realization that his wife is dead and that he no longer has the house he worked so hard for or the car that he loved so much. His wife has been dead for three years now. He still asks daily where she is and when she's getting home. She better not be out shopping again. To tell him that she is dead would throw him into a deep depression. He was told that when he first came to us and the results were devastating. He forgot the words within a few days, but it took almost a month before he was "back to his old self" or the self that we knew, anyway. He spends his day arranging things in their proper place and order, according to his standard, though often we might not agree.

We have builders and farmers, fire chiefs and businessmen. Each of these wonderful men has amazing stories to tell if they can remember them. It's a large part of our job to try to keep those stories as part of their lives as long as it is possible for them. In the end, they will not remember their family members, or their own name, for that matter.

We are like a family. Their loved ones become our loved ones as well. We are now doing for these men what their wives, mothers (yes, some of them are young enough to still have mothers), sons and daughters, in-laws, nieces and nephews, brothers and sisters have been doing, sometimes at home alone with no help for a very long time. It is a unique bond, one we value and honor. To create a loving atmosphere and maintain the dignity of these men and their families is our primary goal and we take it very seriously.

We were happy, enjoying our challenge and feeling rewarded. Life was good!

Then the administration changed. The "team" concept was implemented. Our caring, wonderful head nurse, who had a master's degree and a vast knowledge of geriatrics and dementia, specifically Alzheimer disease, was politically "dumped" for another person who had no concept of dementia or Alzheimer disease and is still trying to learn.

Under our new "team" concept, we now have an evaluation "team." It consists of the superintendent, who on a very rare occasion stops by when dignitaries are in the building to show them "his" Alzheimer/wanderers unit. Also part of this team is a gero/psych (geriatric psychiatric) team who come on what they consider to be a regular basis (maybe once or twice a month) to spend approximately five to ten minutes on a rotating basis with two or three of our vets to evaluate their responses to standard questions and observe their responses to the question and their surroundings and then make recommendations as to what medications should be given or behavior modification is appropriate. Most of their time is spent in the office doing the paperwork. This is not all their fault. Their timetable is also mandated. Also on this team are the director of nursing and her assistant who are afraid to come to the unit, so as a result are rarely seen, the social worker, who comes every day and spends time but isn't allowed much input, and our "Veteran care co-coordinator" who is allowed input but not given much clout.

The superintendent had a floor plan in mind. He positioned the furniture in a configuration he thought appropriate and mandated that it should remain in that position. He hadn't considered that most of the seating areas now faced the door, allowing the men to notice when it was opening and how. The new job of the assistant superintendent (a $70,000 plus a year position) was now to come to our unit several times a day to make sure that the furniture was in its proper place. He was then required, if he did not find it in this position, to move it back again. The main problem with this concept is that furniture moving is one of the Alzheimer patients favorite activities. Our fearless leader was not willing to accept this fact of life, so the saga continued. A floor plan appeared and was posted on the bulletin board. The daily visits to re-arrange the furniture continued much to the amusement of the staff. After about six weeks, he gave up.

The recommendations of the authorities on the Alzheimer resident suggest soft, same-colored walls and floors, and muted furniture to create an atmosphere of calm. A home-like atmosphere is also indicated, but often, I think that the concept of "home" gets lost in all the "specs" and regulations that are set forth when the policies for space are written up.

These regulations require signs indicating where the bathrooms and living spaces are located. I know these things are done to comply with standards set by the State, but doesn't it make sense to ask the people who work with the population and the people who live in the environment every day what might work best before you just do something? I understand the need for signs to inform staff, firemen, and

97

police, etc. But, how these decisions affect the lives of the people who live here should be the first consideration.

Our facility requires that the bathroom doors be kept closed. These doors are labeled "restroom." I'm sure that men of that generation, who, by the way, have dementia, will, when they need to go to the bathroom to relieve themselves, look for a sign that says "restroom" that is placed next to a closed door. Consequently, when they cannot find the "men's bathroom," they are forced to find somewhere else to go, usually in a corner or sometimes on a chair. The staff is always on the alert for signs of the search for the "restroom," but with a ratio of five or six wandering dementia residents to one staff, this task is difficult if not often impossible in such a large space.

Large signs placed outside every door on the unit state the room number printed numerically and in Braille. On these signs are spaces for the pictures and names of each resident in each room so that the guys can see their picture and their name and know that this is their space. A great idea, or it would have been if administration had taken the time to actually take pictures and put them into the frames. Some of our staff took pictures of the vets on their own and put them in the slots. This worked well until administration decided that the frames should be changed and attached to the wall with screws, requiring a special tool to remove the frame and change the picture.

Is the tool kept on the unit where we can change the pictures as residents leave the unit and the faces change?

No.

The head of maintenance has the tool. If administration ever gets around to taking the picture, then sending it to the unit, we must then call maintenance to have the old picture replaced.

Maintenance doesn't come.

This also presents a very definite danger when new staff come to the unit and have to distinguish who is who for purposes of passing medication or prescribing treatments.

The residents should have some say in how their living space should look and feel. Even though their capacity to do so is diminished, they still remember, to some degree, how home should be. Familiar things that are of interest and importance to the people living in this space are just as important as serenity at all costs, or that is the opinion of those of us who work day after day with this population. As Paul Klaassen states in an article in,"Assisted Living Success, "planners are now more aware of the importance of paintings, sculpture and other art works as a cuing device, as well as adding warmth and visual interest to interiors. If every CEO lived in their facility for two days, they would automatically change the environment" (33).

In our facility, we are not allowed to tape anything on the walls (it might remove some of the paint). Most of our walls are bare. In our main living area, which is an expansive space, there is a television, an organ, generously donated by a local

98

music store, a total of four pictures on the walls, several chairs, attractive but institutional-looking, a coffee table and two end tables and a bulletin board on the entry wall and a grease board on an alcove wall. Neat, but not very home-like. I personally think that something pleasing to the eye that will lead the resident from one place to another is more important than touching up the paint. But what do I know; I just work and live with these wonderful people on a daily basis.

Research indicates that artwork of any nature lined consecutively along hallways encourages the resident to "follow the yellow brick road" as it were, to find their way, as Maggie Smith suggests in the Alzheimer's Care Guide (August, 1999).

When we can sneak it by, we line the hallways from the bedroom as a guide to indicate the way to the central living areas such as the dining room and living room.

Through activities, the staff tries to give the residents a way to affect their environment through art and music. Activities are an intricate part of our job and take on many forms. Tracing and cutting out decorations to be placed about in the living space give the guys a sense of whether it is spring or fall. We create flowers, trees with soft green leaves, birds and grasshoppers in the new, green grass on the bulletin board and on the large picture windows when spring appears. When spring turns to summer, there are swimming holes and fishermen, bright sunshine and boating scenes to fill these areas. Fall brings bright colored leaves created by the guys with the help of the staff, followed by turkeys and football. Winter brings snowmen and mittens. Veteran holidays always display patriotic themes. These creative activities not only give the men a sense of making this space their own, but also keep their minds and senses alert. This is productive work to them and keeps them busy as well as stimulated. These things also help to create a home-like atmosphere for our residents. This is what we who work with these wonderful men strive for.

But, the "team," who we never see, makes decisions on some of these matters that are counterproductive to our efforts.

During the Christmas season, on the bulletin board just inside the entrance of the unit greeting me when I came to work after being off for a few days, was a beautiful red sleigh, reminiscent of a time past. It had graceful lines and a high curved back. It sat on runners of gold curled on each end, just waiting to take you on a ride through the snow. The background behind the sleigh was a brilliant, dark blue. It was stunning. Seeing the sleigh there brightened their day. Even though it was 6:00 a.m. three of four guys were up and about. They were sitting in a group looking at the sleigh, talking about it as I came in. "Isn't it beautiful?" one of them said, and the others agreed.

I hung up my coat and began to make rounds. I went into the dining room. What a joy! Red and green twisted streamers were draped from the ceiling emanating from the center of the room, encircling the room. Bright pictures of packages and Christmas ornaments hung between the bright papers. Darcy (one of the 3-11:00 staff) had struck again.

I was thrilled. The guys as they came in smiled and generally perked up, some commenting; for some, their smile said it all. About 11:00, our Veteran Care Coordinator came in. The decree had come down from above. In the dementia/Alzheimer's units, there were to be no Christmas decorations until 2 weeks before Christmas and they were to come down one week after Christmas. Too confusing for the dementia resident. (I'm sure when they were at home, none of their Christmas decorations went up until two weeks before Christmas, aren't you?)

The men watched the decorations come down. The whole atmosphere of the room changed as they asked verbally or by expression, "Why?" Their families came in and asked the same question.

What are we to do? The rest of the building was decorated for Christmas. The TV is showing Christmas programming. The radio is playing Christmas carols and veterans groups are distributing gifts for the season. We are not allowed to decorate or talk about Christmas until December 10th. Does this mean no radio or TV? Will the men not be able to leave the unit, so they will not be confused by the decorations in the lobby or in the canteen? Can they go to church? The chapel is decorated for Christmas.

Whose best interest is being served here? The interests of these brave men who served our country and are now locked away from the outside world for their own safety with bare walls to look at, or those of the "team" who sit in their offices in the "executive suite" and make decisions "by the book" for people that they do not personally know and will never take the time to know.

In our lives, none of the things that are part of the normal living for the Alzheimer victim would be acceptable to us. All the more reason for all of us who work in this field to do anything and everything possible to make the lives of these men, who fought for and risked their lives for us, as happy and comfortable and productive as we can.

Sandy

The selection and training process that Sandy describes at the start of her essay is rigorous; she gives us a detailed sense of how thoroughly the staff is prepared, and a good picture of how they made a Veteran-friendly environment. This strengthens her theme

She then gives us a general idea of the nature of the disease, the character of the residents–and a detailed look at the daily lives of two residents. This gives us a good sense of the quality of care being given the residents, and of their importance and value as human beings. This sets us up quite well for her damning account of the new management team.

100

Hopefully you noticed a few things: the devices of voice she uses to express her disapproval of the new administration; her ironic description of the new administration's activities and policies; and the support her research provides.

Sandy ends her piece with a long description of their efforts to make Christmas enjoyable for the men—and the response of the new administration. This one detailed example establishes her theme and brings her essay to conclusion.

(See the Anthology for more examples of Essay and Memoir.)

7 EXTENDING THE ESSAY/MEMOIR: Researching

An essay or memoir often takes us as far as we need to go in the process of coming to terms with a subject. But sometimes experience isn't enough: we need to know more, reach beyond our experience, perhaps to make plain an issue out of the essay/memoir, perhaps to argue the issue to a satisfying conclusion, perhaps to research in order to gain enough knowledge to secure a tentative conclusion, and perhaps to take a stance or act. Writers of all sorts research, deeply, sometimes for years, in order to know their subjects thoroughly.

In the following piece, which begins with a memoir/essay, the author, Danielle, recounts a vexing situation with her mother, examines it, and gets all sorts of insight into its causes. She makes a correct psychological diagnosis of her mother's condition. But she isn't sure; she isn't aware of the entire psychological pattern or of its implications. So she researches the part that still puzzles her. Two things happen: as she sets her knowledge within a wider context, she confirms her own insights; and she gains further insights.

Asked to comment on the process Danielle talked about her first resistance to writing in a journal. But soon she discovered that she had a real talent for writing. Caring more and more for what she wrote, she found that she had "a whole bunch of feelings to get creative about." In the process she found that the journal helped her realize,

> *all sorts of stuff about myself that I didn't know was there. . . . By the time the final paper was assigned, I knew I had a whole world of feelings to sort through that I could put into story. [She has a subject, her mother, that she could] be passionate about, that was real and important. . . .*

But Danielle couldn't find a way to start. So, she writes,

> *I sat down at the typewriter, closed my eyes, let an image come to me, and wrote it down. This was the memory of my mom hitting me. Immediately I knew the direction I wanted to take my paper before I even finished writing it down. I wanted to write about how I had the chance to get even with her for all those years of abuse. But I couldn't jump from one memory to the next. Each was so important in their separate ways even though they were related in others. So I*

102

decided to talk about how each one made me feel. I thought the best way to make the paper flow was to go back and forth, from past to present (past experience to present thoughts about the experience) to tell my story. I used this weaving technique throughout the whole essay . . . At the end of this paper I still had many questions about my mother that I didn't have answers to. I tried to come up with the best answers I could but I was left wondering.

The suggestion was made that she research manic depression, her first guess as to her mother's syndrome. Danielle writes,

So that's what I did. I collected as much information as I could and took notes on what I thought was important and what I should use in my paper. Once I had the research done, the paper just fell together. I approached it almost the same way as my essay. I thought that the easiest thing to do would be to compare my memories of my mother with what I learned about manic depression. Once again, I used the weaving technique to accomplish this. It was fairly easy to write compared to the essay. But in a way it helped me more. At least in a different way. I finally found some of those answers I was looking for.

When I was done with it, I felt as if a huge weight had been lifted off my shoulders. I could finally move on. I also found that I love to write.

Danielle's memoir/essay/research paper follows.

"Erik, just get out of here!"
My brother and I are having another fight. Usually we fight because he wants me to do something outrageous for him. He always gets his way.
"Erik, shut up! Mom's on the phone. She's going to be pissed! Just shut up!"
Like he's really going to stop screaming. Like he really cares. He's not the one who'll get in trouble. He's not the one who gets yelled at. He's not the one who gets punched.
"I'm telling mom!" And with that said, he slams my bedroom door. That's just great. He slammed the door and he's telling. That's not a good combination. I'm definitely going to get it now.
I can hear my mom on the phone in her room across from mine. The door is closed but I can hear her muffled laughs. It's so strange that she seems so calm and normal. Like the screaming didn't bother her at all. She can be a good actress. But I know the truth. Deep down inside she's full of rage. And I know what's going to happen when she gets off that phone. I just hope the conversation lasts long enough for her to calm down.
In the meantime, I might as well just wait. If she's going to get me, she'll do it. I can leave, but she'll get me when I come back. It will probably be worse if I leave. I might as well get it over with.

103

I don't hear her talking any more. Did she hang up the phone? Maybe I should have gotten out of here. Maybe I should have run—far away.

I can hear her coming. Her footsteps are pounding outside. They're getting closer. Louder. The door flies open.

Brace yourself, Danielle. Cover your face. Tighten up into a ball. "Don't-you-ev-er-slam-your-door-again-do-you-hear-me? Ev-er! I don't want to hear your ugly voice for the rest of the night!"

Well, that wasn't so bad. Maybe a bruise or two on my back or arms. My face will be fine. I can stop crying now; I'm OK. But, God, how I hate her!

***

I think it's amazing how my mind chooses this incident to remember. I've been hit numerous times by my mother, but this one stands out the most. I remember it like it was yesterday. I think I remember this one the most because of how I felt. It was one of my lowest moments. I actually sat there while she hit me over and over. I went through all the motions. All the preparations. What angered me the most is simply that she never asked what happened. Never stopped to talk to me and my brother. She just hung up that phone and went straight for my room. I can't seem to get past the fact that it didn't matter to her. A part of me will always feel like she never cared about me.

My mother was a very controlling person. She liked to get her way. Actually, she had to get her way. And she would get what she wanted at any cost. She made me fear her so much. She hated my dad. (They were divorcing.) I wasn't allowed to talk to him—or whack! She was jealous over my dad's other kids from his first marriage. She actually told me they were my cousins. When I was old enough to realize they weren't, I couldn't see them—or whack! Over and over she told me I was annoying and ugly, and I would never have any friends. I had to come home from school and tell her I hung out with the "popular people"—or whack!

My mother controlled everybody in her life. I think she felt out of control if she didn't. Unfortunately, all she ended up doing was losing everything: her marriage, her family, and any respect she had from people, especially mine. At the same time, my mother robbed me of a great deal of my life. I missed out on having two extra sisters and a brother. I missed out on having my dad around, or even being able to have a relationship with him. I missed out on a family. And I missed out on a mother.

Living with my mother was very stressful. I never knew what kind of mood she'd be in. Mostly she was always angry and depressed. But there were times when she was fine, happy. I would try to do the right thing so she couldn't get angry. I felt like I constantly had to tip-toe around my own house. I never knew what was coming. I lived like this for fifteen years. Then my mother died.

It's ironic how I forgot all this when she died; I can't believe my mind completely forgot it all. I was devastated when I lost my mom. All I could think about was that I had no mother. Who was I going to talk to, and go shopping with? Who was going to raise me? I would never hear her voice again, never see her again . . .

About a month after she died, I realized something—quiet. There was no more screaming, or mean words, or hitting . . . most of all, no more hitting. I didn't need anybody to raise me. Hadn't I been doing that by myself? I didn't want to talk to her. I didn't want to look at her. How could she have been so cruel? I have never been so angry in my life. I hated her. And worst of all, I would never have the chance to repay her for the pain.

I came close once . . .

* * *

"I swear to God, mom, don't hit me! I'm warning you!"

Like that would stop her after all these years. So she hit me. But this time it didn't hurt. Maybe because I was bigger and older. Maybe because I was ready to fight back.

So I hit her. Hard. Square in the jaw. Her eyes widened. Her mouth fell open.

"Come on! Hit me again! I dare you, mom!"

"Don't you ever hit me!" And with that she tried again with a very shaky punch.

"Then don't you ever hit me!"

I was pumped up now. Bam! Square in the jaw again. I was ready for anything. Unfortunately, my mother wasn't. She admitted defeat and swore she would get me later.

I, on the other hand, had never been happier. I realized that moment I had changed. I was on my own. I always had been. I was going to rely on myself. Defend myself. Stand up for myself.

***

It's sad that this is the best memory I have of my mother. Anyway, I felt like I got ripped off. I was just beginning to stand up for myself and then she went and died. We only fought one other time after that. I was just getting started, but never got to finish.

***

After some time went by, a bunch of questions emerged from my anger. I wanted some answers. I wanted to know more about my mother. Where did she get her anger from? Where did she learn to be so violent? Why was she so mean to me?

This was difficult to do without her alive. I knew there had to be much more to my mother's problems. Sure, my dad and mom didn't get along. He even cheated on her, which would piss anybody off. But she was beyond pissed. She was completely out of control.

My mom's family is pretty normal. They are all very loose and they are far from dysfunctional. At least not messed up enough to produce my mother. And when I asked her family if she was ever hit while growing up, the response was a strong no.

The only thing I had to go on was something my dad told me once. He said that my mom was adopted by my grandfather. My grandmother had her before she met my grandfather. And she didn't know who her real father was.

So I started asking questions about their family. When were my grandparents married? How come they waited ten years to have five more children after my mom? What was grandma's family like?

Nothing added up. I do know that my mom was born before my grandmother married my grandfather. The rest of what I know is pieced together from bits and pieces of past conversations with her family, and a little guessing. My grandmother is from Germany. She lived there during all the Hitler stuff. From what I'm told, her brother was a Nazi. Somewhere around the end of the war is when I think she got pregnant. Whatever it was, she was ashamed enough to keep it a secret.

My mother found out about their father adopting her when she was around fifteen. And it was kept a huge secret from everybody. The only people who know today are my Aunt Heidi (because I told her), my brother, and me. My grandparents don't know we know.

I could just imagine how this would have made my mother feel. The person she had thought was her father wasn't. Her real father obviously wanted nothing to do with her. And it was a secret from everybody. I think this is where her problems with rejection and security started.

But that still didn't explain her mood swings. There would be days when she would sleep all day and barely get up to shower. Other times she would be extremely violent. And on rare occasions, she would actually be happy and do things.

I'm starting to think she had a form of manic-depression. Her long low periods and short high periods are strong characteristics of the disease. I only wish I knew for sure. It would make it easier to forgive her. But at least I understand more about her.

Having some idea of what was wrong with her doesn't erase what happened. My mother's problems left scars on everybody. The bad memories stayed with me for a long time. Even now, it's hard to forget them.

I've had to struggle a great deal in order to move on with my life. It wasn't just the physical abuse that I had to get over, but the emotional abuse as well. I had a difficult time thinking well of myself and that I was deserving of any love, even

106

though I wanted that more than anything. I was looking for love from people who would never be able to give it to me; that was the problem. I didn't know anything else but what I was used to.

Fortunately, a loving aunt showed me what it feels like to be cared for, although I didn't change for that reason alone. I'm just lucky enough to have made it through this and come out stronger than before. I would not have my strength, courage, and determination if it weren't for what I went through with my mother. For that, I have to thank her.

For years I struggled with my feelings for my mother. Even today, it's hard for me to forget the misery she brought to my family and me. Her bad moods were impossible to deal with, especially when she took them out on me physically. But now I'm starting to wonder if her problems were completely in her control.

Part of this is because my brother was diagnosed with clinical depression last year. Seeing how this disease took him over and how he is still trying to battle it made me realize two things. The first is that most of the time my mother showed the same traits my brother has. The second is that maybe, like my brother, she couldn't control her moods. The only difference between my mom and brother is that my mother's mood wasn't always predictable. I started to think she might have had a form of depression.

But how could I know this for sure? Since she died four years ago, it would be difficult for me to find out. Having a doctor diagnose her is out of the question now. So I did the next best thing. I took my memories and tested them against research done on depression.

Psychiatrist Donald F. Klein, MD, says, "About one woman in four will experience a depressive disorder . . . " (Gutefeld 86). The odds that my mother may have had depression were already high. But what amazed me was that she had every single symptom I researched.

My mother's biggest activity of the day was sleeping. Dr. Klein says, "Many depressed people fall asleep easily and suffer from chronic sleepiness, while others may have difficulty sleeping at night" (89). There are countless times I remember waking up and hearing the TV downstairs. Night was the only time my mother would usually be up, and she'd always be watching TV. My mother's sleeping habits were completely backwards.

There would be times when nothing would get done in the house for a couple months. Dirty dishes would be stacked on the counters. Clothes would pile up over a period of years. (When the laundry was finally tackled, there were clothes that didn't even fit anymore.) There would be little food because she didn't want to go grocery shopping. The house was a mess. Dr. Klein also says, "Depressed people often feel as if they are always out of gas. Everything becomes an effort" (88).

"Some depressed people, instead of not eating, may find themselves overeating, mainly on sweets" (89). I find this interesting because my mother gained a lot of weight over the years. I hardly ever saw her eat in front of me, but I remember coming home from school on most days and picking up dirty ice-cream dishes and

candy wrappers downstairs where she watched TV all night. Dr. Klein thinks the most important "symptom of depression is increased expression of pessimism" (89). My mother was the most negative person I've ever met. All she did was complain. Why clean up if it's going to get dirty again? Why get up if it's going to be a bad day anyway? She'll never have a perfect family. Everything was hopeless to her.

Also, she treated everybody and everything as a direct attack on her. Everything had to do with her, or so she thought. If my dad came home late, he did it on purpose to upset her. If I got in a fight with my brother, I did it on purpose to upset her. And she was so worried about what other people thought of her. So much that she would tell people lies over the littlest things because she was embarrassed

My brother has these exact symptoms. He acts the same way, but it's not as severe. It's hard for him to do normal, everyday things. It's hard for him to interact with people, especially people outside the family. Through him, I can see how much of a struggle it is just to get through the day. I can understand my mother's struggles a little better.

At this point I would definitely say my mother had depression. But what about the times she would be on a rampage? What about the times you couldn't reason with her over anything? If you got in her way you would be setting yourself up for World War III. This makes me think she might have been manic-depressive.

According to Dr. Klein, "Manic depression is a less common form of clinical depression. It's marked by wide mood swings. There may be periods of frenzied activity followed by periods of 'down days'" (89). In the book, Inside Manic Depression, Charlotte Clark recalls a particular memory of one of her high periods. She talks about her irrational decision to start a business and the result of her hasty actions:

I had no qualifications as a businesswoman. The lack of business training, experience, or more funds, were of complete indifference to me. . . . During each high phase I also felt terribly clever and creative. . . . Two brief months after my thrilling venture opened its doors they had to be closed. The sledgehammer of depression hit again. . . . Again I neglected to do anything to improve my appearance. From morning until night I looked as if I had just gotten out of bed (41).

Charlotte says her husband's, "efforts to reason when I was high were like trying to reform an alcoholic on a binge" (41). I can understand this completely. Trying to tell my mother she was wrong was impossible. I can recall an incident when my mother bought a bunch of cosmetics to sell. She was so involved, for a period of time. No one could tell her it was a bad idea. She knew what she was doing. Even though my dad protested, and said it was a bad investment, she went ahead anyway. She ended up losing her money.

108

Like Charlotte, when my mother was depressed she rarely got up to shower, brush her teeth, or brush her hair. She would sit in the same nightgown for weeks.

Another problem my mother had was spending money we didn't have. Charlotte talks about one of her shopping sprees:

> On that particular day my thoughts raced as fast as the car. . . . I wheeled my bronzed Mustang into a parking spot near my favorite department store. . . . Approval of the charge took some time, but I left unconcerned about that, or the monthly payments (41).

I can remember numerous times my mother took me shopping for clothes, and we spent well over $700, easily. Sometimes she'd come home with bags of stuff for herself. One time she charged up new wallpaper for the kitchen and dining room, and a new tile floor. My dad said,

> She never paid the bills. There were months of unpaid bills stuffed in the kitchen drawer. And there was no way to pay them; that's why I took the checkbook from her. It took me a long time after she died to get out of debt and rebuild my credit.

The personality trait that bothered me the most was my mother's outbursts of anger, which came out verbally and physically. Charlotte says, "One time while manic . . . my smoldering anger burst into flames. [I was] appalled both by words that spewed from my mouth and by the power wielded by them" (21). She continues to talk about the fights she had with her husband. She was on such a high that she was unable to control herself.

A part of me is angry at my mother and doesn't want to use this as an excuse for the abuse I had to deal with. But if my mother had this sickness, I can at least understand why she did the things she did.

But where does manic depression come from? Dr. Klein says,

> There is a strong underlying biological component to the illness. . . Now most experts believe that clinical depression is basically a chemical imbalance in the brain, which may or may not be triggered by stressful life events (Gutefeld 88).

Well, my mother certainly had to deal with some stressful events. Finding out her father wasn't her real father. A shaky marriage. Getting breast cancer, then five years later, colitis. Any of these could trigger depression. Pennsylvania psychologist, Martin Seligman, and others, indicate that "'learned helplessness'— or believing one can't influence one's destiny—is a major factor in depression" (Peele 67). I think my mother felt that her destiny was always out of her control.

109

So did my mother inherit this or did life's problems cause it? Technically I'll never know. Since her mother's side of the family doesn't have any documented cases of mental illness, and since I don't know who her real father was, it's hard to tell. But if my brother has depression, maybe it was something in her genes that was passed down.

"Like heart disease, like cancer, like any sickness—if depression is not treated promptly and effectively, it can kill" (Gutefeld 86). My mother never killed herself, but I think depression took a toll on her body. She ended up with colitis, ulcers in the colon, and it eventually led to her death.

It's unfortunate that something like this can take over a person's life and the lives of others around them. Maybe if my mother had had some help earlier, things would have turned out different.

Danielle

Bibliography

Clark, Charlotte. Inside Manic Depression. San Marcos: Sunny Side Press, 1993.

D. Lee. Personal Interview. 12/3/96.

Gutefeld, Greg. "Depressed Persons." Prevention. Sept. 96: 86-91.

Peele, Stanton. "Behavior Genetics." Psychology Todav. July, Aug. 95: 50-68.
183

With her memoir Danielle gets into her subject immediately, recounting the classic event of her life with mother: another inexplicable beating. She brings us into it, describes all the particulars that count. It's happened dozens of times; she knows the pattern thoroughly. But this one memory points up how irrational the beating is. This becomes her subject. What will explain this? Mother was a control freak. But that doesn't explain why Danielle feels robbed of her life, and why life with mother was so crazy.

Before Danielle can figure it out, her mother dies. This seems a great loss—at first. Then the first of several revelations comes home. Life is now quiet; the screaming and hitting have stopped. How could mother have been so cruel? And now she can't get back at her. But she did, once. She recounts that event, her only means as a near adult to counter her mother's irrational, abusive behavior.

But getting back, even a little, isn't enough, and all the questions remain. Where did mother get her anger? She explores her family history. All her leads give at best partial clues, but some understanding. Her mother was illegitimate, a family secret. Maybe this created feelings of rejection and insecurity. But it didn't explain her mood swings.

110

Mother's mood swings are still a puzzle. Maybe they were a form of manic depression. If that were the case it would be easier to forgive her behavior. Danielle does want to forgive, and put this behind her, but she's not going to be satisfied until she can understand the situation more thoroughly. She sums up her thinking so far: her mother's pervasive effect on the entire family; her own difficulty thinking well of herself; and where the love of an aunt—and her mother's abuse—have left her personally. But she persists; and that is the mark of good essay and research.

Unanswered questions remain, and she's exhausted her own experience and expertise. She begins to research the subject—without settling for easy answers. She will pursue this until she's satisfied.

Danielle first summarizes the situation and her questions, then brings the matter to one basic question: Did her mother really have control over her behavior? Her brother's behavior, clinically diagnosed as depression, seems to provide an answer. How can she know for sure? She reads authorities on psychological illness; a world of knowledge opens to her, confirming what she had suspected. She goes back and forth between the main features of this new knowledge and her experience of her mother. Confirmation of depression comes again and again. Her brother's symptoms further confirm the label.

But she's not done. What about the mood swings, the rampages? She brings in other readings. The manic-depressive pattern, though more rare, holds for her mother. She researches manic-depressive behavior in terms of her mother's behavior, especially the outbursts of anger, the most vexing and harmful of her mother's behaviors. She gets answers; her mother's pattern is manic-depressive. But she is still reluctant to forgive her. The unstated implication is that perhaps her mother could have controlled of her behavior.

She researches further: where does manic depression come from? If it's genetic, perhaps it's not her mother's fault after all, and not within her control. Danielle's research leaves her with the possibility that mother's behavior was out of her control—but it's not conclusive. Danielle leaves it at that, and with some generosity of spirit turns to her mother's untimely death: too bad that her mother couldn't have gotten help in time.

Danielle thought the subject through. Going beyond her own experience and expertise, she chased her questions down one by one, reasoning them out, researching family history as best she could, and consulting the experts. She got answers to her questions. Though her guesses are accurate, she was not satisfied until she *secured* them. And with that, "a huge weight had been lifted off [her] shoulders." Research—the rewards are not few.

The following piece is also a research paper, but in the form of a letter to the author's father. The letter also embodies the characteristics of a memoir, a personal essay, an explanatory essay, and a research paper that gives him both new knowledge, and secures insights held tentatively.

I won't comment following this paper. Within the essay the author comments on its creation and on the writing and research process. And the casual tone of the letter/research paper gives us a very clear picture of what he's doing, and how. But as you read, observe his tone of voice, humor, use of understatement, irony, (gentle) sarcasm, and the repetitions that bring his points home. Note especially his use of the repeated, "coincidentally you were drunk," to burn in his theme.

Dear Dad:

Yes dad, it's me. How are you? It's been a long time since we talked and even longer since we saw each other.

I haven't talked to you lately because when I tried calling the other day the phone wasn't working, but I know that it has been fixed; I'll call you soon. How is everybody over there? It's been a while since I read the e-mails that you sent me.

I don't know if I have written you a letter before. I think not. But now I'm writing you for a very delicate reason and to cover a matter that maybe I should have left buried. It's something I have to analyze in order to determine the magnitude of damage that this could cause to me in the future. It sounds as if I were suffering from a serious virus or illness but in reality it's nothing like that . . . or maybe it is.

Briefly I'm going to tell you how this letter or paper started (because its also a paper for my English class). In my English class we had to carry a journal through the semester, where we would write everything we wanted to. At the beginning it seemed to be nonsense and the truth is that I gave little importance to all that I wrote. That was until I got to the fifth paper of this class, which had had to be created from the main point of the journal. It means that the idea was to read the journal trying to find something, a detail, a person, a situation, etc, that could be considered as the theme of the paper due to its presence in most of the entries. Trying to find this "something" in all the entries led to some surprises. I was very surprised not only because there was one general aspect but also because this one aspect was something like: the desire of being and having everything that I couldn't have or be in Colombia.

Well, there's nothing extraordinary so far, right dad? The weird thing came later when I started thinking about my drive to succeed and where this inclination or obsession to succeed had come from. Without going too far I realized that what propels this is my desire to show You how excellent and accomplished my life can be. When this was clear, one more question arose: Why do I want to show, precisely You, how successful I can be? I know you are my father but I feel this same need towards my mother, so I felt deep inside that there was another reason. I knew, though, that I wouldn't find this answer through you or my family, so based on what I've learned on how parents influence kids (I wrote a paper about this), I

112

tried to find an answer in the memories that I have of our relationship when I was little. And surprise! It was there.

Do you remember how you said to me all the time that I wouldn't be anybody in the future with my attitude and personality? Do you remember that? Well, this constant phrase was recorded inside of me and today is one of the motors that helps me move forward.

But again there was something that felt incomplete; a detail was missing. Coincidentally, during those days I had a dream about you being drunk and saying that I was nobody. That obviously opened my eyes and I easily remembered that you used to say things like that to me when you were drunk or when you had a terrible hangover. Indeed, all this information took me to the writing of the fifth and sixth papers in which I tried to explain all the terrible fights that we had when you were drunk. And in fact, these papers awoke a tremendous interest in me to know why my family, and you, never accepted that you had a problem with alcohol, why I buried such a big part of my childhood in order to not be hurt by the memories, why I left home when I was only 17 years old, how all the memories of an alcoholic father affect my life.

I understand that at this point you must be surprised and confused because I have never talked about this. Besides, some of these things may not make any sense, but that's exactly the idea of this letter or paper, to explain all these things to you—and me.

I want to tell you the way this writing works. This is called a "research paper" and as its name indicates, the idea is to find information that could answer a question or support or refute an opinion. Now that it is clear for you how I got to this paper, let's move on to the principal theme: alcoholism.

The points to be studied are (and I'm sorry to sound rude but I'm going to call things by their names, Ok):

1. Prove that you were (or continue to be?) an alcoholic no matter what you or my family says about it.

2. Prove that most of the negative experiences in my childhood were due to your alcoholism and were not "situations that every kid is supposed to live with," as my siblings would say.

3. Discover if these memories from my childhood affect me now, and if there's a possibility to overcome the negative effect that they could be having on me.

Now let's get started. Oh, before that, let me tell you that the information that is going to be here wasn't made up by me; it was found in books or articles written by people who know about alcoholism, OK. So don't think I'm just inventing all this stuff to support my thoughts, which might appear to be false as well.

1. Proof of your alcoholism: I read many questionnaires to tell if a person is or is not an alcoholic but I think they all make no sense. According to those tests, basically every body who has drunk by themselves and forgotten about what they did when they were drunk is an alcoholic. I know that for the purpose of this paper

I need information more forceful so I found a paradigm developed by Burgan (1974) (Middelton-Moz, Dwinell 9) that illustrates the real alcoholic person.

[The referenced drawing is not included here, but is explained in detail below.]

The way that Jane Middelton-Moz and Lorie Dwinell explain this figure is as follows:

In figure 1, (the person) is nauseated, irritable and hung over. In figure 2, (the person) is warm and responsive, having drunk enough alcohol to alleviate the withdrawal symptoms. In figure 3 (the person) has had enough to drink to be in the rising side of a blood/alcohol curve (and) is expansive and intoxicated. In figure 4 (the person) is on the falling side of a blood/alcohol curve and is drunk, depressed and irritable. In figure 5 (the person) is passed out. (11-12).

Does this sound familiar to you dad? Remember how this would occur week after week. I still can see you as figure 1 on Saturdays or Sundays' mornings. You looked awful when you were hung over. When I was very little I remember everybody in the family trying to be quiet to not wake you up because we knew you would be upset. As I grew up I just decided to stay in my room those mornings waiting for you to wake up to come to my bed to start arguing about the first thing you could come up with. Sometimes you argued about my friends, who you never liked, or sometimes you wanted me to clean the house, or sometimes you yelled at me for getting home late the night before. Every thing with only one purpose: to bother me. Usually from Sundays' nights to Wednesdays you were a normal father (unless you decided to drink those days, which was actually very common. You would be home early; would bring us gifts, you know, candies, toys, sometimes clothes; would be nice to us and my mom. You would be a great father those days.

On Thursdays I can see you as figure 2 when you would go out sometimes and have a couple of drinks but still be warm and nice. After this, hell would come up on Friday and, Saturday nights where you fit in figures 3, 4, and 5. I never understood how you were so happy when you were drunk and the next minute you would be mad at everybody for no apparent reason. I always told you that it was ok to drink if you didn't get upset, but first, it never happened and second, now I understand that you couldn't control these changes of mood; it was the alcohol that had control over you. At some point when you were drunk you were extremely affectionate. You would kiss and hug every body and say that you loved us so much and bla, bla, bla. Five minutes after, you would be fighting with me or my mom about money or the lack of communication in the family or any other stupid thing that you thought of. Then when you were tired of screaming, yelling and breaking things like plates, glasses or mirrors, you would go to the pink sofa, which for some

114

reason was your favorite, and finally pass out till the next day. Just to start over again.

Do you think that that is enough to prove that you were an alcoholic? I think it is. Oh, by the way, let me just tell you briefly all the harmful effects alcohol can cause you according to the DuPage County Health Department:

> *Overuse of alcohol can affect memory, distort mental perceptions, affect social relationships or job/school performance, interfere with physical coordination and have adverse effects on many organ systems in the body. Heavy drinking is also associated with increased risk of cancer, liver cirrhosis, heart disease and pancreatitis.*

2. Proof of the influence of your alcoholism in most of the negative situations fill my childhood: I know now that there are three characteristic problems in an alcoholic family or in any other dysfunctional family that cause or represent negative memories. The three problems are lack of communication, resistance against the traumatic situation and the leaving of home at an early age.

2.1. Lack of communication: "Alcoholic families demonstrate poor problem-solving abilities," (Connecticut Clearinghouse); "communication is often non-existent (and) often this lack facilitates the alcoholism. Always it maintains it" (Perez 64).

How many times was the TV more important than a conversation in our house? TV was always the most important thing. I think that the dinning room table was only for decoration because all of us used to eat in our bedrooms while watching TV. We never talked. But Why? Because you were closed to accepting communication with the rest of the family members (Perez 64). Yes dad, you thought you were always right. I remember that when I was 12 I wanted to talk to you about the new experiences I was having with drugs and alcohol, or about all the piercing I wanted to get in my ears, or about how good I was doing at school, or about the way I felt about you drinking so often. But I never did. I was scared because I knew you wouldn't understand and instead you would just get upset. I was right.

When I pierced my ears I wore a bandana for two days so you couldn't notice them, but one day when I was sleeping in your bedroom you got home and as soon as you saw the piercings in my ears you woke me up with tremendous smack. Coincidentally you were drunk. When I felt that I was so pissed, I stood up and tried to hit you back; but my uncle who was there that night stopped me, so I just cursed you. You couldn't do anything about that because my uncle was there and apparently you didn't want him to see the violence that used to take place in our house.

I started drinking when I was 12 and at that time I used to get drunk every weekend. You never noticed this because you were always drunker than me when I got home, or you had just passed out. One day, when I was throwing up and you

115

finally noticed that I was drunk, you hit me with your belt; my mom was begging you to stop. I said to my mom, "don't worry ma, let him be happy." Coincidentally you were drunk. When you got tired of hitting me that night you left the bedroom along with my mom and I went to bed. Before I fell asleep I cried for a long time.

I started doing drugs when I was 13. When I was caught at school with pot, they sent me home and they called you at work to tell you. I was scared as hell waiting for you to get home. I thought I was going to get beaten up. When you got home you didn't hit me; you only made me understand that you were disappointed. You were disappointed? Funny. Coincidentally when you got home you were drunk. At the end of your long speech on drugs, etc, I went to bed and I cried, reproaching myself for having disappointed you and my mom.

Although my grades were always the best, I was kicked out of school when I was 14 years old because according to the principal I didn't have any respect for authority (this is also a problem shown in children of alcoholics that I'll discuss later on). When the principal told you what had happened, you said: "It's OK son, everything is going to be alright." What? I was surprised by your reaction. You seemed to understand that this could happen to any kid. You told me that day that maybe I was too good for that school. I felt so happy for having such a good father. I know that that day you weren't drunk or anything like that. You showed me understanding and love. The next day you got drunk and said to me that I deserved being expelled from school because of my disrespectful attitude. You said that I had disappointed you once more.

Every time you were drunk I tried to tell you that you needed help—that you were an alcoholic and needed professional help. As soon as I realized that talking with you about alcoholism when you were drunk wasn't a great idea I was like: "Alright, I'll talk to you tomorrow." Then the next day I would try to talk to you but you were hung over and didn't want to know about anything. I kept on repeating this same process over and over. Your answer was always the same: "Leave me alone."

Now, do you think that's enough proof to say that there was a tremendous lack of communication? I know it is. What I don't know and I'll probably never get to know is how things would be if I would have been able to talk to you about my problems and your problems. I don't know if you became an alcoholic for this lack of communication or if this was just a consequence of it. I know, though, that since every family member was scared of talking to you, you found in alcohol a refuge from the indifference of all of us.

2.2. Resistance against the traumatic situation: "Children in alcoholic families usually develop their own internal "buffer" to traumatic events. Events that render them helpless at five almost seem to be taken as expected occurrences at age eleven" (Middelton-Moz, Dwinell 14). After the process of trying to deal and talk to you without any success, I just gave up. I spent most of my life in my bedroom when I was 15 not wanting to interact with anybody in the house. I would be around the house all day but as soon as I heard the "ring" of the door I would just

116

go to my room and lock the door. I didn't care about you or anything related to you.

Although things were no longer unexpected, it doesn't mean that they didn't hurt. It hurt when you were fighting with my mom and I felt so powerless. It hurt when you were listening to very loud music in the middle of the night, not letting me escape reality through my dreams. It hurt to eat alone every night. It hurt to not talk to you.

So the time went by between TV and books till my nerves exploded sending me out of home.

2.3. Leaving home: I tried to leave home three times. At this point I believe that you don't remember that. I had almost forgotten about those awful moments. Do you want me to tell you how they occurred? OK. Here I go.

I was 14. One day you were hung over fighting with my mom about money because she was blaming you for not contributing economically to maintain the house. You were so loud I couldn't sleep so I left my bedroom to see what was going on. You were about to hit her. Immediately I jumped over you and knocked you down. For some reason I felt so strong that I could hold you in a way that you weren't able to move. I remember you telling me to let you go, and I also remember my words: "Please dad, stop doing this. Can't you see that we all love you and that seeing you in this way is very, very painful." After this, you couldn't say anything. I stood up, went to my room, packed my suitcases and left. You didn't say anything at all. My mom tried to stop me but I told her I was going to be OK and she believed me. I went to my grandma's house but she said I couldn't stay there because she didn't want to be in the middle of the way that you wanted to educate me. I ended up coming back home after two weeks due to my mom's pleas.

I was 16. One day I got home too late after a party. You were there waiting for me. When I came in you tried to lock the door behind me. I knew instantly that you were drunk and that you wanted to beat me up so I told you that I wouldn't let you touch me again. I pushed you and I left the house running. When I was outside crying and walking without direction I heard you coming yelling and running. I started running too and I kept on running and running, and even though I knew you weren't following me anymore I just couldn't stop. I ran from you, from the hell of my house, from my childhood. I stayed at a friend's house for a while but after one week I ended up coming back home because of my mom's pleas.

You know what? It's funny that after I went back home those two times you just pretended nothing had happened. There were never promises of change, no regrets, no "I'm sorry," no nothing.

I was 17. I just couldn't stand you anymore but I knew that if I wanted to escape from you, I would have to go to a place where you couldn't find me. Many adult children of alcoholics move "thousands of miles away just in case" (Middelton-Moz, Dwinell 64). I also went far away. Very far away. I realized that the only choice I had to leave home was going to a different country. Thank God, *my sister gave me a hand. Finally with the pretext that I was going to the United States to make enough money to go to school, I left home to never go back.*

So well . . . those are a few very representative examples of what my childhood was like. A childhood that passed by between silences and fears, between screams and tears, TV and books, dreams and reality, between hopes and hopes.

Climates such as these promote insecurity. Climates such as these promote a sense of isolation and of never having been loved. Climates such as these promote a poor sense of self worth. Children of alcoholics come to negate the worth of their own love and feel unworthy of anyone else's. For many the giving and taking of love becomes a mystery. The feelings of insecurity, the ineptness with love, and the low self-esteem are the major reasons that these children as adults exhibit a veritable host of debilitating personality traits." (Perez 118).

This brings me to the third part of my letter.

3. The effects of being an Adult Child Of an Alcoholic (ACOA) and the possible solutions: When I tried to find out what an ACOA's personality is like, I freaked out to see that there were at least 25 characteristics that distinguish us. Of course I don't have all of them because, as Joseph F. Perez writes, "In some children of alcoholics, some of these characteristics are dominant, in other children barely discernible, and in still others some of these characteristics do not exist at all" (118). I'm just going to tell you the ones that I fit, in order to find solutions for them and furthermore to understand the aspects of my life that I have to pay particular attention to.

3.1. "Adult children of alcoholics over-react to changes over which they have no control." (Geringer 44). The point that Janet Geringer is trying to make here is that since "the young child of an alcoholic was not in control" during his/her childhood, when growing up he/she needs to turn that around and become a kind of control freak (44).

I always try to have complete control over my life. Knowing this, I trust myself more than I trust anybody else because most of the time I consider that other people's opinions will be against mine or will ruin my life. If I make a plan or a decision and things don't result as they were expected, I not only get upset but also I overreact and consider that to be the end of the world.

Four months ago, my girlfriend and I went to see a concert. They didn't let me in because I was 19 years old and you had to be 21 at least. That for me represented the end of the night. Although my girlfriend didn't care and she even tried to convince me to go somewhere else, I felt like I had ruined her night and my night. Afterwards I just told her to not talk to me because I was pissed and I didn't want to be mean to her.

Now that I think about this and about so many examples that come to my mind, I see clearly how overreacting to changes over which I have no control, controls my

118

life. As Geringer writes, "Something like this has happened many times before, usually in childhood. It brings back all the plans that were never carried out, the promises that were never kept, and the punishment that [I] could not relate to [my] crime" (75).

3.2. "Adult children of alcoholics constantly seek approval and affirmation" (Geringer 44). This basically means that I consider any affirmation sketchy. Since the messages in my childhood were so mixed ["Yes, no, I love you, go away" (Geringer 45)], every time I hear a compliment, especially at work, I have a hard time accepting it because I think there's something behind it. I think that they are trying to gain my trust so they can attack me later somehow. After a while I realize that they are just trying to be friendly. It happens to me all the time.

3.3. "Adult children of alcoholics are either super responsible or super irresponsible" (Geringer 47). Thank God I'm super responsible. Janet Geringer explains that children of alcoholics try to "please parents, doing more and more and more" (47). That's very true. All my life I have been responsible because I have wanted to show that to you. Even now I try to do great at school so that at the end of each semester I can call you to tell you how good my grades are. I consider this something awesome and maybe one of the few good characteristics of an ACOA. Therefore I don't want to find any solution. I'm obsessed with being responsible; I just am and if it implies my desire for showing you my success, it doesn't matter.

I also found out that among those few good characteristics that I owe to my experience in my childhood are: "higher intelligence and communication skills, achievement orientation, a responsible and caring attitude, a positive self-concept and a more internal locus of control and self-help" (Dupage).

Nevertheless I still need solutions for the other two "problems" that I fit as the child of an alcoholic. Actually they are very simple. Knowing that those two problems exist (which is a 90 percent of the solution) I can now "increase [my] awareness of over-reaction" or distrust (Geringer 76). And then understand that there are many things in life that I can't control but that this doesn't mean that's the end of the world. And finally take the risk to feel support and encouragement from the people around me.

Before I move on to the conclusion of this letter let me tell you briefly that I have found from my own experience one more problem related to your alcoholism. It is the lack of respect for authority. This is because you represented the image of an abusive authority and I associate authority with abuse. This has represented so many problems for me. That's why I was kicked out of school and that's why I got fired from my last job. I'm trying to correct this, and now with all the information I have obtained through this paper, I know I'll get to do it.

Nevertheless dad, I'm here now and I consider myself a survivor. As Ackerman writes, "without their level of resilience where would they be now? If it were not for their ability to take control, accomplish tasks at an early age and only depend upon themselves, how could they survive childhood" (Ackerman 1)? I had two options, either go crazy and blame everybody or deal with this by accepting, forgiving and letting go. I took the second choice; and now, dad, to end this long letter I just want to say that I have nothing against you, because I understand that you were sick and that you never meant to hurt me. Above all, with few, but beautiful examples you showed me that you loved me. Y yo tambien te amo. (And I also love you.)

Rodrigo Castillo Mahecha

Bibliography

Ackennan, Robert J., Let Go and Grow Recovery for Adult Children. Pompano Beach, Florida: Health Communications, Inc., 1987.

"Alcohol, Health. Children of Alcoholic Parents." Nov. 2002 http://www.alcoweb.com/english/gen_info/alcohol_ health *society/alco social_* env/family/ children.html

Connecticut Clearinghouse, "Children of Alcoholics. Important Facts." http/www.ctclearinghouse.org

DuPage County Health Department, "Alcohol and Drugs." http://www.dupagehealth.orglmental_health/alcohol_abuse_2.html Steinhausen,H.

Geringer Woititz, Ed. D., Adult children of alcoholics. Pompano Beach, Florida: Health Communications, Inc., 1983.

Middelton-Moz, Jane Lorie Dwinell, After the tears. Pompano Beach, Florida: Health Communicatios, Inc., 1986.

Perez, Joseph F. Coping with the Alcoholic Family. Muncie, Indiana: Accelerated Development, Inc., 1986.

"Objective" Writing and the Symbolic:

If it's true that we transform much of what we see to personal concerns, what's to keep that automatic, mental process from intruding into "objective" writing: a paper on literature, history, or science, a report, the description of a patient or a work situation?   What's to keep your mind from transforming that material symbolically to your personal concerns? Nothing. It happens all the time (often without notice) in biographies, histories, essays—and yes, even in reports and scientific papers. "Projection" is the common psychological term for it. "Bias" is another, but it's what the mind does all day long to make sense of our own lives.

What's to keep you from projecting yourself unaware into your "objective" writing? Nothing, but your ability to see it happening. That awareness won't come instantly; it will take time to see what your own mind is doing. And that awareness won't necessarily keep you from projections. But it will give you a basis for seeing what's happening in your writing and for acknowledging the part you play personally. That is one mark of "objective" writing; it is aware of the personal and acknowledges its part.

The two papers you've just read example the idea. Danielle and Rodrigo could easily have fallen into the "projection" trap. But with close attention to their images, and thorough research, both have come to an objective perspective on very personal situations. They know where they are personally, and have given a troublesome mother and father their due.

8 EXPLORING STRUCTURE: the Elements of Movement and Connection

This chapter may at first seem like a contradiction to the book. Why bother examining the structure of sentences and paragraphs if sentence structure comes to us naturally, and as the linguists tell us, is embedded in the mind? Why bother with structure if it comes naturally with *writing*, as you've seen in the pieces you've been reading, writings done for the most part without conscious awareness of structure?

First, and last, it's important to get the *feel* of structure as you begin a first draft. As you learn the elements of structure you will get a sharper feel for it. Then you can take more advantage of structural devices—as you write—without interrupting the natural process. And with this awareness you can analyze a first writing to see how you've put it together, and clarify sequences that aren't clear or where the "voice" feels wrong, which should save you time and anguish.

Besides seeming like a contradiction, this chapter may also feel like, well, school. I was introduced to sentence diagramming back in grade school, but I found it intriguing, even fun, discovering what made a sentence work.

Now sentence diagramming might take it too far; but the model we'll work with stays close to home, and keeps close company with common sense.

Paradoxically, the elements of structure are something to learn—then forget in the first writing, like musical scales. Scales are the base of every musical phrase. Structure is the base of every sentence. But you don't have to think structure or scales when you're writing or playing, just get the feel of it.

I'm going to recommend that you have pen and paper in hand as you read, so that you can play with each element, in writing, as we go. Yes, play with it, in writing. Nothing else will make it clearer, give you a better feel for it, and make it yours.

The Elements of Movement and Connection

Here's a tightly structured start. Bear with me for a little; this will take concentration, though the model is quite basic.

I'll be working with four fundamental terms as simply as possible: topic/periodic and coordinate/subordinate. I'll add another, very common term: "statement," the understanding of which is not universal. But it's basic (very basic) to understanding structure.

122

Structure is essential to all writing: four elements of structure, two of movement, topic and periodic movements; and two of connection, coordinate and subordinate connections.

That last sentence would look like this, structured in outline form, the increase in numbers showing increasing levels of specificity, or detail. (This is just outline form, and would usually be: I, A, 1, a, 1), a), etc. I think numbers alone are simpler).

1 Structure is basic to all writing:
    2 four elements of structure,
       3 two of movement,
          4 topic and periodic movements; and
       3 two of connection,
          4 coordinate and subordinate connections.

This is a "cumulative sentence" (more later). If you look at it for a minute, some things stand out, like the parallel character of levels 3 and 4. Here's how it works.

- The statement at level 1 anchors the sentence, states its subject.
- The phrase at level 2 comments *directly* on the level 1 statement, specifies what is meant by "structure."
- Each phrase at level 3 comments *directly* on the preceding phrase at level 2—but not on each other. They specify the four elements.
- Each phrase at level 4 comments *directly* on the preceding phrase level 3— but not on each other. They specify movement and connections.
- A higher number indicates more specificity or detail.
- The levels are defined (separated) by marks of punctuation.

Let's take it bit by bit, first with a simple two-level sentence.

The topic movement with simple coordinate (parallel) connections

1 The dog has gotten into the garbage again—
2 cigarette butts and ashes coating the overturned garbage bag,
2 cans strewn about the floor,
2 the smell of rotting tuna salad lingering in the air,
2 black banana peels hanging out of an empty milk carton.   *Maryann E.*

Notice the features. A *statement* at the top, level 1, anchors the sentence and gives us the main idea. Four phrases at level 2 detail the particulars of that

123

statement. This is the **topic movement**: the phrases comment on the **top** sentence and look to it for meaning. The connections at level 2 are **coordinate (parallel) connections,** here, a list of like things. All the items at level 2 comment *directly* on the level 1 statement.

A first principle of structure operates here:

Statements anchor sentences, sentence fragments, and paragraphs and give them meaning; without a statement, meaning is absent.

This first principle comes with two implications: 1) With a statement a human being has stepped into the sentence (or paragraph) and *said* something; 2) Without a statement, a sentence contains only items—without human comment, and without meaning. A statement has a subject, and a human saying what the subject does or is. Subject and verb (and object), right? But it's easy to think that an infinitive or gerund as a verb, which would make this paragraph's first sentence read like this: "The first principle coming with two implications . . ." Notice the difference? "Coming" leaves us hanging; "comes" doesn't. Statements have a definite feel.

- *Suggested Writing: Take a minute or so to write a few, simple, topic/coordinate sequences.*

The periodic movement with coordinate connections

Now *reverse the **movement*** of the previous entry so that the anchoring statement comes at the end (Maryann's original writing).

2 cigarette butts and ashes coating the overturned garbage bag
2 cans strewn about the floor,
2 the smell of rotting tuna salad lingering in the air,
2 black banana peels hanging out of an empty milk carton—
1 The dog has gotten into the garbage again.   *Maryann E.*

The **movement** is now **periodic,** the statement coming at the end (like the period). The periodic movement has a different feel than the topic movement; the topic movement says: here is the point, specifics will follow. The periodic movement reverses this: here are the specifics, the point will follow.

Note that with the phrases at level 2 we have no statement of meaning—just items. Meaning is suspended until the statement at level 1 arrives. The periodic movement gives us particulars to take in and think about until a statement comes along to tell us what to think or feel.

- *Suggested Writing: Take a minute to write a few periodic/coordinate sequences.*

124

The topic movement with subordinate connections

Look again at the **topic movement**, this time with **subordinate connections.** With a topic/subordinate movement, each level comments *directly* on the level before, getting more specific, level by level.

> 1 *I am full of disgust —*
> 　2 *ninety-pound people who are wrinkled with age,*
> 　　3 *lying on their sides and perhaps half off the bed,*
> 　　　4 *in that position for hours and sometimes days*　　　*Camille*

With **a topic movement**, again, we're told at the start what to feel about this situation. It's disgusting, that's it. But the connections are **subordinate**. Each level is more specific, *each* phrase commenting directly on the phrase before, and all phrases—through each preceding phrase—commenting on the level one statement.

- *Suggested Writing: Take a minute or so to write a few topic/subordinate sequences. (Notice the difference from the coordinate sequence.)*

The periodic movement with subordinate connections

Reverse the movement to make it a **periodic movement** (Camille's original writing, Chapter 1).

> 　2 *Ninety-pound people who are wrinkled with age,*
> 　　3 *lying on their sides and perhaps half off the bed,*
> 　　　4 *in that position for hours and sometimes days. . .*
> 1 *I am full of disgust.*

Again, the feel of the piece changes with this **periodic movement**. Instead of stating at first that she's disgusted, Camille has in effect opened the door and drawn us with increasing detail into the scene with the patients, **subordinately**.

Here's the principle involving movement and connection:

> ***2. Movement FROM the anchoring statement is topic; movement TO the anchoring statement is periodic. Connection is either subordinate or coordinate. An extended sentence can mix these four elements.***

- *Suggested Writing: Take some time to write a few periodic/subordinate sequences (again noting the difference from the coordinate sequences).*

The Periodic movement with mixed connections

Camille's original paragraph, complete, **mixes connections** within a **periodic movement**.

> 2 *Ninety-pound people who are wrinkled with age,*
>> 3 *lying on their sides and perhaps half off the bed,*
>>> 4 *in that position for hours and sometimes days,*
>> 3 *some of them weeping softly to themselves,*
>> 3 *others lying with such apathy.*
> 1 *I am full of disgust.*
>> 2 *Lethargic and weak fearing everyone they meet.*
> 1 *My stomach just churns.*

The movement is still **periodic,** the statement at the end. But the subordinate sequence is broken after level 4; two more **coordinate (parallel)** phrases are added at level 3. How do we know they're coordinate? Look at the content: the phrases don't comment on each other; each comments *directly* on the phrase at level 2. "Weeping" doesn't comment on "lying." And "lying with such apathy" is about apathy, not "weeping" or "lying on their sides."

How else are we given notice of coordination? (Take note.) In each phrase the actions are introduced by the same word endings, "ing" endings (gerunds): lying, weeping, lying. *Coordination is always marked by similarity, the repetition of word endings, words, and phrases.* Keep that in mind; it's a basic element of clarity.

Observe that with "Lethargic and weak . . ." we're into another periodic sequence looking towards the statement, "My stomach just churns," which is coordinate with "I am full of disgust" at level 1.

The rhythm of this periodic sequence is hard to miss: the particulars, a statement; another particular, a statement. Strong, isn't it.

Clear use of coordination is one mark of good writing.

Why do we need to be given particular notice of coordination at the end of a subordinate sequence? Because—unless we *are* given notice—we expect the subordinate sequence to continue, that Camille will continue to talk about the *position* of the inmates. But she doesn't; she talks about weeping.

Here's the principle:

> *We expect a subordinate sequence—unless we're given notice of a coordinate sequence with introductory words, phrases, or word endings that are identical or parallel in form.*

- *Suggested Writing: Take some time to write a few periodic/mixed sequences. Introduce your coordinate phrases, using the same words, word endings, or phrases.*

126

The Topic Movement with Mixed Connections

Making use of the different character of **topic and periodic movements** and of **subordinate and coordinate (parallel) connections** is a prime mark of strong writing, writing that knows where it's going. Getting the *feel* of these four elements lets you put them to use *as* you write. Being *conscious* of these four elements allows you to edit a piece that doesn't—yet—know where it's going.

Here's an example of **variety within a topic/mixed sequence,** which is a nicely written "cumulative sentence," the style of major 20th Century authors.

> *1 She was wild,*
> > *2 running barefoot up grassy hills,*
> > *2 skating down hills without protective gear,*
> > *2 laughing wickedly at the boys,*
> > > *3 who dared not cross her,*
> > > *3 who did not fight her,*
> > > *3 who did not want her body,*
> > > > *4 young, thin, shapeless, and boyish.*   *Tu Le*

This **topic movement mixes subordinate** and **coordinate (parallel) connections.** Call it a **topic/mixed sequence.** With the topic movement we have a statement at the start. With the subordinate sequence (levels 1, 2, 3, & 4) we get into specifics, detail. With the coordinate sequences (levels 2 and 3) we get the intensity of her wildness: "running, skating, laughing"; and "who dared, who did, who did." Notice of coordination is given at level 2 with the repeated "ing" (gerunds again); and at level 3 with the repeated "who:" "who dared not cross her," who did not fight her," "who did not want her body." These repetitions make for emphasis, heightened emotion, as repetitions always do. Note the richness of the details at level 4: "young, thin, shapeless, and boyish."

Mixing movement and connection

In the following sentence both movement and connection are mixed.

> > *2 Smart,*
> > > *3 Mt. Holyoke College-created,*
> > *2 and smartly dressed in a maroon suit,*
> > > *3 with sand-dollar-like buttons,*
> > > *3 and expensive silk,*
> *1 she sat,*
> > *2 sure of herself,*
> > > *3 empress,*
> > > > *4 monolith.*   *Tu Le*

First we get the details of her intelligence and outfit, then the statement that positions her, and then the status implied. Lots of information is packed into this sentence. The full richness and complexity of writing involves the varied use of these four elements.

- *Suggested Writing: Write a few sentences in which movement and connection are mixed.*

Mixing movement and connections at the paragraph level:

This variety of movement and connection also works at **the paragraph level**, as Camille's writing on the nursing home illustrates, and the following piece as well. I'm now identifying levels of both phrases and statements, but I'm doing it, as before, between marks of punctuation.

> *3 Maybe my coolness turns people away.*
> *4 People say I'm conceited,*
> *4 but I know that's not true;*
> *2 I am just the coolest person around.*
> *1 I am super cool.*
> *3 When it is one-hundred degrees outside,*
> *2 I still need a windbreaker.*
> *3 When the temperature drops around the seventies,*
> *2 I bring out my corduroys and sweaters.*
> *3 When it is around the forties,*
> *2 I break out the winter apparel:*
> *3 Eskimo coat, ski mask and boots, and my trusty thermal underwear.*
> *3 Don't ask about when it drops below twenty.*
> *2 I am practically out of commission.*   *Nathan Edge*

"I am super cool," topically anchors the entire coordinate sequence at level 1. But in order to get to that statement, periodically, Nathan has to do a little thinking: does my coolness turn people away; am I conceited? No, I am cool. Actually, I am super cool.

Nathan then (level 2) gives us four examples of "super cool," each one cooler than the next. All the sentences starting at level 3, begin with "when," which gives us notice of coordination, as do the statements at level 2, beginning, "I still, I bring, I break, I am."

Notice the structure. The "when" *phrases* at level 3 look to the level 2 *statements* to give them meaning (to anchor them). "When it is one-hundred degrees outside, . . ." leaves us suspended. "I still need a windbreaker," puts us on solid ground, completes the idea.

128

The paragraph has a very clear structure, coolness intensifying with the coordinate structure as it goes. I don't suppose Nathan planned this out; I guess he felt it coming as he thought about "super cool" and found the metaphors: if he's super cool, he's got to dress warmer as the weather gets colder.

Structure is embedded in the mind and occurs naturally in writing—especially when we can feel it coming, and bring it along.

- *Suggested Writing: Write a few paragraphs in which you are using first simple topic/coordinate and subordinate sequences, then periodic/coordinate and subordinate sequences, and then mixing the movement and connections. Identify levels by statements (sentences mostly) as the illustrative paragraphs below do. Don't break sentences into levels unless they have more than one statement.*

Look at a longer piece, two paragraphs, illustrating all the features of movement and connection discussed. Try to get a sense of the structure as you read, especially Joanne's use of coordinate (parallel) structures.

> *Picture yourself not existing, really; think hard about it—to no longer exist. To not be able to touch anymore, to feel things rough and smooth, things that prick and bring blood forth. To not be able to smell, the fresh flowers in the summer, the cool crisp air in the winter; to pass a store and smell the baked pastries just placed on the counters. To not be able to hear, laughter, giggles, whispers and screams, or someone telling you, "I love you," or the sounds escaping from the radio. To not be able to see all the colors, the blues, reds, greens and yellows that make you want to smile. To not be able to see the sun, the moon, the falling star.*
>
> *Existence is nothing but our senses. How sad we are without them. How sad it must be to not exist. I hope, when I die, life beyond will be as beautiful as this one. I love my life, can't do without it.*
>
> *Joanne Piekut*

Is this piece periodic or topic in movement? Where is the anchoring statement? What words/phrases introduce the coordinate connections? Here it is in the numbered outline form.

> *2 Picture yourself not existing, really;*
> * 3 think hard about it—to no longer exist.*
> *   4 To not be able to touch anymore,*
> *   5 to feel things rough and smooth,*
> *   5 things that prick and bring blood forth.*

4 To not be able to smell,

    5 the fresh flowers in the summer,

    5 the cool crisp air in the winter;

    5 to pass a store and smell the baked pastries just placed on the counters.

4 To not be able to hear,

    5 laughter, giggles, whispers and screams, or

    5 someone telling you, "I love you," or

    5 the sounds escaping from the radio.

4 To not be able to see all the colors,

    5 the blues, reds, greens and yellows that make you want to smile.

4 To not be able to see the sun, the moon, the falling star.

1 Existence is nothing but our senses.

  2 How sad we are without them.

  2 How sad it must be to not exist.

    3 I hope, when I die, life beyond will be as beautiful as this one.

    3 I love my life, can't do without it.

Joanne begins with a topic she wants to picture and think about (periodically): "not existing." She doesn't have a conclusion, a statement to anchor the piece; first she's got to explore the thought: existence and the loss of senses. She explores the thought, coordinately, through all five senses with "to not." Then, periodically, she arrives at her conclusion (level 1).

Coordination is clear as a bell—but for two places. Did you feel a little glitch at the first level 5 sequence, "to feel," and the second level 5 sequence, "to pass?" All the other level 5 phrases are introduced by: "things," "the," "laughter," "someone." All of them are things, not actions, as "to feel" or "to pass" are.

The glitches are easily fixed by removing "to feel" at the first level 5; and by removing "to pass a store and smell" at the second, level 5 sequence.

Joanne, obviously, did not plan her structure; if she had, the two glitches would have shown. But for the most part she must have *felt* the rightness of coordination, "To not be able . . . ," and the lists following. Just the *feel* of structure is often enough. But a little more *awareness* of structure doesn't hurt.

Perhaps you noticed that the "To not be able . . ." sentences are actually sentence fragments. With a colon after "no longer exist" and semicolons dividing the 4/5/5 units, most of the piece would become a long, "cumulative sentence." (See below.) A (very) long cumulative sentence might be a bit much to take in. Sentence fragments make the reading a bit easier without the necessity of starting a new sentence for each phrase, which would be cumbersome, and ruin her rhythm.

Three principles govern structure. A fourth principle identifies the character of subordination and coordination

> *1. Statements anchor sentences, sentence fragments, and paragraphs and give them meaning; without a statement, meaning is absent.*
>
> *2. Movement FROM the anchoring statement is topic; movement TO the anchoring statement is periodic. Connection is either subordinate or coordinate. An extended sentence can mix these four elements.*
>
> *3. We expect a subordinate sequence—unless we're given notice of a coordinate sequence with introductory words, phrases, or word endings that are identical or parallel in form.*
>
> **4. Subordinate structures give specifics, detail; coordinate structures give emphasis, heightened emotion, through repetition.**

Without these links at each level, writing begins to fall apart; meaning goes missing or is vague. With these links, sentence to paragraph to finished piece, meaning has a clear structure.

Principle three can be taken as the default principle: the subordinate sequence takes care of itself, doesn't need to be given special notice; but the coordinate sequence needs notice, a signpost, a road sign, a flag: Dear reader, turn here.

PS—On repetition: It should be obvious by now that the repetitions, which define coordinate structures, are always emphatic. You've seen this throughout the book. Repeat a word or phrase and you have emphasis. Recall J. F. Kennedy's famous speech; "Ask not what your country can do for you; ask what you can do for your country. Ask not . . . ask . . ."

There is a downside to this, which I'm about to illustrate. There is a kind of repetition that calls attention to what you *don't* want emphasized. There is this deadly, boring, repeated use of: there is, it is, he could, they would, he, she, it, usually at the beginning of sentences. These repetitions draw attention to themselves, like it or not—and kill "voice." There is (oh, sorry).

One way out is to find your subject, something beyond "it, there, he, she" etc. Then find verbs more descriptive than "are, is,' and the like, which give your subject existence, no more.

Sentence fragments are also a way out, as is the cumulative sentence. Read on.

The Structure of the Cumulative Sentence

The cumulative sentence is identified by Francis Christensen (*Notes Toward a New Rhetoric*) as 20th Century style, the way sentences are written by some of our best writers of fiction and nonfiction: Ernest Hemingway, William Faulkner, John Steinbeck, Eudora Welty, Robert Penn Warren, Rachael Carson, H. L Mencken, Lionel Trilling, Mark Van Doren, Edmund Wilson, and the like.   Francis Christensen writes,

> *1 The main clause . . . advances the discussion;*
> *1 but the additions move backward, as in this clause,*
>> *2 to modify the statement of the main clause,*
>> *2 or more often to explicate or exemplify it,*
>>> *3 so that the sentence has a flowing and ebbing movement,*
>>>> *4 advancing to a new position and then pausing to consolidate it,*
>>>>> *5 leaping and lingering as the popular ballad does (5).*

The cumulative sentence has the character of the writing that I've been encouraging, and using as illustration, writing that is "dynamic rather than static, representing the mind thinking," as Christensen puts it (6). Rather than demanding up front a well-structured, complex sentence, the cumulative sentence gives the mind space to think: first to make a statement, think about it, add a particular, think about that, add another particular, etc., and then go on to the next statement. Citing Montaigne, Christensen concludes, it's "the art of being natural."

The cumulative sentence has another benefit: reducing anxiety, since it goes a step at a time: a general statement—what next? A detail—and next? Another detail. Is that all I want to say? Maybe. Etc. You don't have to have it all in mind at the start. Observe the process in the next entries.

> 1 *The Greek howls with laughter,*
>> 2 *roars till tears come down his face,*
>> 2 *till he's choking on cigar smoke,*
>> 2 *till the whole damned table is laughing with him,*
>>> 3 *pounding fists, hands, bottles,*
>>> 3 *laughing and laughing;*
>>> 3 *and I'm laughing right with them.*   *E. Flynn*

132

1 The folds of my jeans are now haven to the soft, furry moth—
   2 a small moth,
   2 my favorite color,
      3 a light beige-grey,
   2 with a brush for a mouth
   2 and gold tipping on the end of his wings
   2 and gold brushed legs.   *Joan H.*

1 I sit on the floor of a smallish dance studio,
   2 curled in the corner,
      3 knees pulled to my chest
   2 a notebook propped against my knee caps,
      3 blue corduroy front and back,
      3 doubled black spiral binding,
         4 the bottom edge resting on a pillow of fat.   *Shara*

1 The only times the bed does not get made is when the owner is having a
"rough day" as her roommate describes it,
      2 one in which the owner knows that right after classes finish she is going to
      run right back and hop under the blue comforter and plush pillows,
         3 a blue comforter that has the ability to keep one warm on the very cold
         nights,
         3 but also to keep one just right on the not so cold nights,
         3 and pillows that give the feeling of sleeping on clouds.   *JB*

   2 Even though what we had is gone and lost forever,
1 you will always have a place in my heart, forever—
   2 as a friend,
      3 (even though we don't talk anymore),
   2 as a companion
      3 (even though we're not that anymore),
   2 but most of all as a memory,
      3 because you can never take that away from me;
         4 what I mean is, that is mine forever.   *KharaWozniak*

1 Never stop to look back,
   2 to cross something out,
   2 to wonder how to spell something,
   2 to wonder what word or thought to use, or
   2 to think about what you are doing.

Peter Elbow, theorist-practitioner,
on freewriting

133

Each of these sentences begins with the main statement, which is developed in detail through coordinate and subordinate phrases, lots of specifics and detail packed into the sentence. Some of the sentences depend heavily on the coordinate sequence, for emphasis; some depend heavily on the subordinate sequence, for specifics, details.

Beyond looking at sentences illustrating 20th Century style, I have another reason for introducing the cumulative sentence; its structure is perfectly parallel to the structure of the explanatory paragraph (and of the explanatory paper as a whole).

The Structure of the Paragraph

The following sequence, a **topic/mixed sequence,** is punctuated as a paragraph, though all the phrases are sentence fragments following the statement at level 1.

1 Feelings from my childhood start to surface.
   2 Feelings I've successfully suppressed for twenty years.
   2 Feelings that I have convinced myself didn't exist.
      3 The emptiness of a house where four people live but no family life exists.
      4 No communication.
      4 No sharing.
      4 No caring.
         5 A mother who works to get away from a life she hates.
         5 A father who shows no feelings—no emotion. Never has anything to say.
         5 A brother who bums around and gets in trouble with the police.

                                           J.

Just the addition of commas would make this paragraph one long cumulative sentence, but with less emphasis on each of its specifics. The structure—as it stands—is that of a paragraph, which brings us to the point: explanatory paragraphs (and sometimes descriptive paragraphs) are structured like topic/mixed sequence cumulative sentences, the anchoring statement coming first, the specifics following.

The following two paragraphs depend largely on the subordinate sequence. The first is a subordinate sequence, the second is a subordinate sequence up to level 7 where it becomes coordinate. [Levels of structure will be defined by *statements* rather than phrases as I've done with the cumulative sentence. Each *statement,*

134

including those within a compound/complex sentence, will be treated as a separate level of structure.]

1 *Omit needless words.*

    2 Vigorous writing is concise.

        3 A sentence should contain no unnecessary words, a paragraph no unnecessary sentences, for the same reason that a drawing should have no unnecessary lines and a machine no unnecessary parts.

        4 This requires not that the writer make all his sentences short, or that he avoid all detail and treat his subjects only in outline, but that every word tell.

William Strunk and E. B. White
from The Elements of Style

1 We need another and wiser and perhaps a more mystical concept of animals.

    2 Remote from universal nature, and living by complicated artifice, man in civilization surveys the creature through the glass of his knowledge and sees thereby a feather magnified and the whole image in distortion.

        3 We patronize them for their incompleteness, for their tragic fate of having taken a form so far below ourselves.

        4 And therein we err, and greatly err.

            5 For the animal shall not be measured by man.

                6 In a world older and more complete than ours they move finished and complete, gifted with extensions of the senses we have lost or never attained, living by voices we shall never hear.

                    7 They are not brethren,

                    7 they are not underlings;

                    7 they are other nations, caught with ourselves in the net of life and time, fellow prisoners of the splendour and travail of the earth.

Henry Beston
from The Outermost House, 24,25

Notice the nicely crafted cumulative sentence at level 6; and the emphasis given with the coordinate structures at level 7.

The following paragraphs are mixed subordinate/coordinate sequences. These paragraphs also present an approach to writing that has kept me good company, and given encouragement and direction as I wrote the book.

1 It is strange to me that as English teachers we have come to accept the idea that the language is primarily learned as speech, is soaked up by osmosis from society by children—
1 but that we then assume the writing down of this flexible language requires a study of linguistics, a systematic checking with lists of standard practices, and so on.
2 Now I realize that we possess many canned arguments about prescriptions versus description,
2 and we share many nuances, having written and taught;
2 but I want to take a definite position as a writer,
3 and my main plea is for the value of an unafraid, face down, flailing and speedy process in using the language.
4 Hence my title, "Writing the Australian Crawl."

William Stafford
From Writing the Australian Crawl, 22, 23

Just a reminder: the complex topic sentence contains two statements at level 1, the "but" creating a coordinate opposition, which puts both statements on the same level.

1 Punctuation—just one of the "mechanics" of writing, after all—is not the first thing you turn to . . . so let me try to keep you here by announcing, quickly, the not unimportant claims to be made.
2 First, manuals of style and college handbooks have it all wrong when it comes to punctuation
3 (good writers don't punctuate that way);
4 there is, I propose, a system underlying what good writers, in fact, do:
5 it is a surprisingly simple system;
5 it is a system that enables writers to achieve important—even subtle rhetorical effects;
5 it is even a system that teachers can teach far more easily than they can teach the poorly systematized rules in our handbooks and style manuals.

John Dawkins
from Teaching Punctuation as a Rhetorical Tool
(CCC 46.4/December 1995)

1 I have grown fond of semicolons in recent years.
   2 The semicolon tells you that there is still some question about the preceding full sentence;
      3 something needs to be added;
         4 it reminds you sometimes of the Greek usage.
   2 It is almost always a greater pleasure to come across a semicolon than a period.
      3 The period tells you that that is that;
         4 if you didn't get all the meaning you wanted or expected, anyway you got all the writer intended to parcel out and now you have to move along.
         4 But with a semicolon there you get a pleasant little feeling of expectancy;
            5 there is more to come;
               6 read on;
                  7 it will get clearer.

Lewis Thomas
from Notes on Punctuation

The Structure of Groups of Paragraphs

The main idea of a paragraph can carry into a second paragraph (or a third) that is subordinate to the main idea. In the two paragraphs below an example forms the second long paragraph.

1 Horace's summary of the purpose of literature, "to delight and instruct." Is also not a bad summary of the purpose of science and nature writing.
   2 The difference is not so much that a science essay gives more weight to the second infinitive as that it unites the two. The best science writing delights *by instructing.*
      3 A good science essay, like any good essay, must be written with structure and style,
      3 but the best science essays accomplish something else.
         4 They give readers the blissful click, the satisfying aha!, of seeing a puzzling phenomenon explained.
         ¶*5 A good example of what I have in mind comes from my days as a graduate student. Not from an experience in graduate* school *but from an experience living in the kind of apartment that graduate students can afford.*
            6 One day its antiquated plumbing sprang a leak, and an articulate plumber (perhaps an underemployed PH.D., I feared) explained what caused it.
               7 Water obeys Newton's second law.
               8 Water is dense.

8 Water is incompressible.

9 When you shut off a tap, a large incompressible mass moving at high speed has to decelerate very quickly.

10 This imparts a substantial force to the pipes . . .

Steven Pinker
from the Introduction to The Best American Science and Nature Writing

Following the above writing, Pinker presents a writing by a ten-year-old girl, explaining that Gordon Allport, the great Harvard psychologist, used it as a model of clear diction for his Harvard graduate students. (This piece covers three paragraphs.)

1 The bird that I am going to write about is the Owl.

2 The Owl cannot see at all by day and at night is as blind as a bat.

¶1 I do not know much about the Owl, so I will go on to the beast I am going to choose.

2 It is the cow.

3 The Cow is a mammal.

3 It has six sides—right, left, an upper and a below.

4 At the back it has a tail on which hangs a brush.

5 With this it sends the flies away so that they do not fall into the milk.

4 The head is for the purpose of growing horns and so that the mouth can be somewhere.

5 The horns are to butt with, and the mouth is to moo with.

4 Under the cow hangs the milk.

5 It is arranged for milking.

6 When people milk, the milk comes through and there is never any end to the supply.

7 How the cow does it I have not yet realized,

7 but it makes more and more.

3 The cow has a fine sense of smell;

4 one can smell it far away.

5 This is the reason for the fresh air in the country.

¶3 The man cow is called an ox.

4 It is not a mammal.

4 The cow does not eat much, but what it eats it eats twice, so that it gets enough.

5 When it is hungry it moos,

5 and when it says nothing it is because its inside is all full up with grass.

138

The following piece consists of three paragraphs, all developing the initial idea.

1 A writer is not so much someone who has something to say as he is someone who has found a process that will bring about new things he would not have thought of if he had not started to say them.

2 That is, he does not draw on a reservoir;

2 instead, he engages in an activity that brings to him a whole succession of unforeseen stories, poems, essays, plays, laws, philosophies, religions, or— but wait!

¶*3 Back in school, from the first when I began to try to write things, I felt this richness.*

4 One thing would lead to another;

5 the world would give and give.

3 Now, after twenty years or so of trying, I live by that certain richness, an idea hard to pin, difficult to say, and perhaps offensive to some.

4 For there are strange implications in it.

¶*5 One implication is the importance of just plain receptivity.*

6 When I write, I like to have an interval before me when I am not likely to be interrupted.

7 For me, this means usually the early morning, before others are awake.

8 I get pen and paper, take a glance out of the window

9 (often it is dark out there),

8 and wait.

9 It is like fishing.

10 But I do not wait for very long, for there is always a nibble—

11 and this is where receptivity comes in.

12 To get started I will accept anything that occurs to me.

13 Something always occurs, of course, to any of us.

14 We can't keep from thinking. . . .

William Stafford
from Writing the Australian Crawl (17, 18)

This next piece, two paragraphs, develops a short, suggestive sentence.

1 First, life is long and college is short.

   2 Very few of our students will ever have to write academic discourse after college.

      3 The writing that most students will need to do for most of their lives will be for their jobs—and that writing is usually very different from academic discourse.

        4 When employers complain that students can't write, they often mean that students have to <u>unlearn</u> writing they were rewarded for in college.

          5 "[E]ach different 'world of work' constitutes its own discourse community with its own purposes, audiences, and genres.
6 The FDA, for example, produces documents vastly different from those of the Air Force;
6 lawyers write in genres different from those of accounts"
(Carolyn Matalene, Worlds of Writing . . .)

   ¶5 But to put the argument in terms of writing that people have to do is to give in to a deeply unwritterly and pessimistic assumption—held by many students and not a few colleagues, namely that no one would ever write except under compulsion.
6 Why should people assume without discussion that we cannot get students write by choice?

      *7 In my view the best test of a writing course is whether it makes students more likely to use writing in their lives: [**Note the cumulative sentence developing.**]*

         8 perhaps to write in a learning journal to figure out a difficult subject they are studying;
8 perhaps to write poems or stories for themselves or for informal circulation or even for serious publication;
8 perhaps to write in the public realm such as letters to the newspaper or broadsides on dormitory walls [or blogs].

Peter Elbow
from "Reflections on Academic Discourse:
How It Relates to Freshmen and Colleagues"
College English, Volume 53 Number 2, February 1991

The topic/mixed structure works from sentence to paragraph, to multiple paragraphs, and also, by extension, to a complete writing. Paragraphs are linked by their topic sentences and sometimes by sentences at the end of a paragraph linking to the topic sentence of the next paragraph. The entire sequence is anchored to a single statement at level 1.

The Structure of an Explanatory (Academic) Paper

If the cumulative sentence is structured like a paragraph, and the paragraph is structured like a complete piece, then the topic sentences of each paragraph, together, would make a paragraph outline of the piece, something like an abstract. Following is a paper on the predator/prey arms race, preceded by a one-paragraph outline. **[I have analyzed the entire paper for structure. I'll make comments on the structure in bold type within brackets.]**

1 [The] concept of co-evolution is known as a predator-prey arms race.
   2 Specifically, an arms race exists when the predator develops new weaponry to overcome the anti-predator behavior of their prey, which in turn develops new anti-predator behavior.
      ¶3 This concept of an arms race is the focus of a recent study of garter snakes (*Thamnophis sirtalis)*, which have evolved to resist tetrodotoxin, the poison emitted by newts (*Taricha)* to avoid capture by their garter snake predators.
      ¶3 Another example of arms race is found between horned lizards and harvester ants.
      ¶3 Australian broadhead snakes also had to adapt to their prey's anti-predatory behavior.
¶1C [Conclusion] An arms race is the ongoing cycle of adaptations of prey vs. predator.

Anti-predator Behavior is Only a Short-Term Fix!
When predators evolve to conquer preys' anti-predator behavior.

2 Prey will do just about anything to avoid getting eaten, while predators will do what they must to get a meal.
   3 If the prey evolves to avoid the predator, the predator evolves to be able to catch its prey. **[These two sentences, using everyday language, invite us to her paper and lead into her thesis.]**
1 This concept of co-evolution is known as a predator-prey arms race.
   2 Specifically, an arms race exists when the predator develops new weaponry to overcome the anti-predator behavior of the prey; and their prey, which in turn develops new anti-predator behavior. **[And these two sentences give us her thesis and its necessary specifics. The rest of her paper will specify and example these points.]**
      ¶3This concept of an arms race is the focus of a recent study of garter snakes (*Thamnophis sirtalis)*, which have evolved to resist tetrodotoxin, the poison emitted by newts (*Taricha)* to avoid capture by their garter snake predators. **[The connection of her first example to her thesis is obvious.]**

141

4 The poison used by newts is a potent neurotoxin that paralyzes its predator by blocking the voltage-gated sodium channels in the nerves and muscles of the organism, causing them to shut down and, thus, placing the animal at risk of respiratory failure (Geffeney, 2002).

¶5 This anti-predator strategy of newts makes it difficult for the snakes to capture their prey.

6 However, the snakes have evolved resistance to the toxin emitted by the newts.

7 Through this adaptation the snakes are now able to capture their prey without the risk of becoming paralyzed.

8 This adaptation, however, imposes a cost. The higher resistance the snake has to the poison, the slower it will move.

9 This trade-off may or may not be beneficial; it depends on the environment in which the snake lives.

10 Being slower may put the snake at great risk to its own predators.

11 Thus the degree of adaptation determines the cost: less to eat, or a greater chance of being eaten. (Geffeney, 2002) **[Cristina takes some pains to thoroughly example here thesis, then caps her explanation with every day, "eat" and "eaten" language.]**

¶3 Another example of an arms race is found between horned lizards and harvester ants. **[She breaks her subordinate sequence with an obvious notice of coordination: "Another example."]**

4 Harvester ants have a poisonous sting and strong bite that makes them a dangerous prey to consume.

5 However, the ants' anti-predator behavior does not seem to phase horned lizards because they have evolved a mucus membrane that covers their throat, stomach, pharynx, mouth and which in turn prevents the poison from being harmful.

6 The predatory lizard immediately incapacitates the ant and binds it with mucus.

7 This physical characteristic evolved in response to the ants' poison. (Eimermacher, 2004) **[By now we're familiar with prey/preditor adaptation, so she doesn't need to remind us of the general principle.]**

¶3 Australian broadhead snakes also had to adapt to their prey's anti-predatory behavior. **[By now we're ready for another example, so she doesn't need to tell us that we're getting one; just the change of subject** from lizards and ants to broadhead snakes is enough notice to break the subordinate sequence and give us notice of another coordinate example.]

    4 Broadhead snakes feed on velvet geckos, which have learned not to enter a rocky area if the scent of a broadhead snake is present.

      5 Because the geckos' anti-predator behavior was affecting the snakes' eating behavior, the snakes evolved a new strategy to capture their prey:

        6 Broadhead snakes now can stay sedentary for long periods of time to reduce their scent on the rocks, in response to the velvet geckos learning to avoid the rocks (Schwenk).

¶1C [Conclusion] An arms race is the ongoing cycle of adaptations of prey vs. predator. **[The mention of "arms race," is enough to take us out of this subordinate sequence back to her thesis, and remind us of her examples and their connection to the thesis.]**

    2 The goal of both prey and predator is to survive the arms race.

      3 Therefore, they must undergo an evolutionary change in order to survive.

        4 Garter snakes have developed a physical resistance to Tetrodotoxin in order to consume the newt.

        4 Similarly, horned lizards have developed the mucus to protect itself from the harvester ants' poison.

        4 Australian broadheads, too, have developed a sedentary trait to hide their sent from suspecting prey. **[With a sentence each, she pulls in her three examples; and reminds us, next, of her basic points.]**

          5 All these reptiles have developed a trait to counter attack their prey's anti-predator behavior.

          6 This co-evolution is an arms race between prey and predator in the battle for survival.

Cristina Vieira

Bibliography

Eimermacher, T. *Coevolution in Reptiles*
   http://www.venomousreptiles.org/articles/177 May 12, 2004

Geffeney, S., Brodie Jr. E.D., Ruben, P., Brodie III E.D. *Mechanisms of Adaptation in a Predator-Prey Arms Race: TTX-Resistant Sodium Channels* Science (2002) 297: 1336-1339

Schwenk, K. , Sherbrooke, W.C. *Mucus-Binding of Dangerous Prey by Horned Lizards* Univ. of Connecticut; Southwestern Research Station, Amer. Museum of Natural History

The thesis of Cristina's paper seems clear, almost simple, by the time we've read through the piece; but that's due to her clear, direct sentences, using simple terms adequate for the subject; and it's due to her transparent structure, especially her use of detailed examples. The argument is not particularly simple: prey evolves to avoid being eaten; predator then evolves to be able to eat the prey, which evolves further to avoid being eaten, each using complex biological mechanisms. But even these complex mechanisms are explained using clear, direct language.

Each subordinate statement picks up clearly from the statement before, with the repeat of a term or phrase, and with the use of words reminding us that she is specifying the sentence before: "this," "specifically," "however," "because," and "therefore." Her coordinate statements, also, are clearly identified: "for example," "similarly," "and," "also," and "too."

This seems a small thing, but often is the difference between a reader (or yourself as writer/reader) following the train of thought, or getting lost. With the use of linking terms you are more conscious of your developing thought; so is your reader.

The structure of the entire paper couldn't be clearer. Papers you write may involve more complexity than this one, but the underlying principle is the same: the entire paper needs to read like a well structured paragraph, which should read like a well structured cumulative sentence.

I'd like to sum up the discussion of structure with two quotes: the first, a cumulative sentence, employing a 2-level coordinate sequence; the second, a paragraph, the heart of which is a cumulative sentence.

In this first paragraph Francis Christensen is summing up his argument for the cumulative sentence, which operates naturally using the senses to think, and which is opposed to a purely rational, intellectual mode of thinking.

1 To this mode of thought [rational, intellectual thought] we are to trace almost all the features of modern literary education and criticism,

> *2 or at least of what we should have called modern a generation ago [the late 1800s]:*
>
>> *3 the study of the precise meaning of words;*
>>
>> *3 the reference to dictionaries as literary authorities;*
>>
>> *3 the study of the sentence as a logical unit alone;*
>>
>> *3 the careful circumscription of its limits and the gradual reduction of its length; . . .*
>>
>> *3 the attempt to reduce grammar to an exact science;*
>>
>> *3 the idea that the forms of speech are either correct or incorrect;*
>>
>> *3 the complete subjection of the laws of motion and expression in style to the laws of logic and standardization—*
>>
>>> *4 in short, the triumph, during two centuries, of grammatical over rhetorical ideas.*

Francis Christensen,
(quoting Morris W. Croll in *Notes Toward a New Rhetoric, 17*)

Rhetorical ideas and practice triumph when writing is allowed to take a natural path.

The philosopher Susanne Langer, within a single paragraph, sums up the basic requirements for discourse.

1 Literal, logical thought has a characteristic form, which is known as "discursive" because it is the form of discourse.

> *2 Language is the prime instrument of thought,*
>
> *2 and the product bears the stamp of the fashioning tool.*
>
> *2 A writer with literary imagination perceives even this familiar form as a vehicle of feeling—the feeling that naturally inheres in studious thinking,*
>
>> *3 the growing intensity of a problem as it becomes more and more complex, and at the same time more definite and "thinkable," until the demand for the answer is urgent, touched with impatience;*
>>
>> *3 the holding back of assent as the explanation is prepared;*
>>
>> *3 the cadential feeling of solution,*

145

3 and the expansion of consciousness in new knowledge. **[Note the cumulative sentence ending here.]**

4 If all these phases merge in one configured passage, the thought, however hard, is natural;

4 and the height of discursive style is the embodiment of such a feeling pattern, modeled word by word, on the progressing argument.

5 The argument is the writer's motif,

5 and absolutely nothing else may enter in.

6 As soon as he leads feeling away from the motivating thought to (say) mystical or moral reaction, he is not supporting the process of understanding.

Susanne Langer
from Feeling and Form, 302

At the third level 2, Langer begins a long cumulative sentence. I've shown its structure, the heart of her paragraph, capturing complexly and beautifully the rhythm of discursive thinking.

Langer brings us back to where we began: writing as "a vehicle of feeling"; with discursive writing, a feel for the developing argument. A "problem" grows more complex, but more "definite and 'thinkable,'" the writer anxious for an answer, but holding off, working sentence by sentence toward a solution until the problem resolves itself in new knowledge.

The mind works naturally and constantly toward solutions, new knowledge. Writing is a marvelous means for focusing and concentrating the ongoing activity of the mind. To be aware of structure is to be conscious of the shape thought takes, your mind, thinking.

It comes down to getting the feel, the flow, of a writing in progress, and staying with the current.

9 ANTHOLOGY

This anthology of student memoir/essay is meant to supplement the memoir/essay chapter, but with a difference. Instead of detailed commentary, I'll ask a few questions. By now you've got fair expertise in the close reading of essay. See what you can discover. Hopefully the different forms that these essays and memoirs take will spur your imagination, widen your writing options.

The following memoir recounts a drug trip taken through the course of an entire day. The author recalls the trip, sensitive to his full experience of it.

I dropped the hit at nine, and waited. Strummed my guitar. Listened to the radio. Smoked a cigarette. I see tracers on the cigarette.

It's kicking in. No turning back now. I head to the Home Ave. Bridge to wait for Hal. When I walk out the door I'm dazzled by the blue sky and bright sun. What a day for a trip.

I get to the bridge, and Hal's not there. It's ten already. Where is he? Can't sit still. I'm wired I smoke a cigarette. Here he comes.

"Well?" he says.

"Shit," I say, and laugh. He laughs too. "You're going, aren't you?"

"Yeah." I hand him his tab, he drops it, and we move on towards Pat's house.

Pat's ready, he drops, and we head for the woods. We walk along Madison Ave., smoke, and talk of nothing in particular. We stop at White Hen for smokes and orange juice. (Vitamin C enhances colors.) Finally, we hit Thatcher and turn into the woods.

Late October. The woods are draped in yellow, orange, red, green, and countless nameless shades between. We stop at the cathouse. We open the orange juice, and drink deep. Pat and Hal sit on the bench, and I climb up top to sit on the roof Pat and Hal talk below me, but I can't hear what they say. I look at the sky. The sunlight condenses into one, concentrated beam. Brilliant, but blinding. I look at the woods. The tree branches move. The woods do their version of the wave.

I clamber down and rejoin Pat and Hal. We move along the path towards the Pavilion. The sunlight showers red raindrops on the river, and the leaves reflect intricate patterns of distorted colors on the water.

"Oh shit," Hal says. "Oh shit, man. Oh shit." He's kicking in now, feeling it heavy. We walk through the woodsy wonderland, and Hal hugs a tree. I roll in the leaves. I find a purple flower, which I put in my ear.

"You're crazy," Pat says.

"You're fighting it," I say.

We come to the field at the Pavilion. A man flies a blue and yellow kite. A plane flies overhead, and a bird makes its way over the field Kite, bird and plane merge into one flight. I want to join in, but Hal and Pat are making their way across the field and I run to catch up with them. We take a break midway across the field to take in the surroundings. We sit in a circle and stare and shake our heads. The grass-covered earth breathes up and down, and above, the blue sky swallows us. So close we could touch it. Butterflies dance across the field, and Hal grabs one as it goes by. We pass around the orange juice like a flask of wine. We spill it on ourselves and laugh uncontrollably. I howl, rolling around on the grass. Tears fall down my cheek as I attempt to catch my breath. We regain composure, and get up to walk to the trestle. "My b---," says Pat, "are all over this field." This sets us off again, and I fall on the ground with laughter. Finally I get up to walk. I walk the path from the trestle to this field everyday, but now the woods are a hopeless maze of trails, and I wait to follow Pat.

The imposing trestle looms over the river ahead of us. Pat scrambles up the hill and down to the woods on the other side to start a fire. Hal and I sit by the river and light up smokes. I skip a rod across the river and watch the water settle after it. Whoops. Almost burnt my hand. I feel nothing in my hands and it's easy to forget there's a cigarette there. Hal rocks back and forth talking to himself. "Take it easy, Hal," he says. "Just take it easy." Along the path under the bridge a lady approaches with a Doberman. Petrified, we scramble up to the tracks. The tracks extend in front of us with no end in sight. Pat shouts to us and we spot him easily in the woods below by the tie-dye he is wearing.

Pat is working on a fire, and I sit down on a log some twenty feet away from him. I want to help build the fire but I'm pinned to the log by the pounding in my head and the numbness in my body. Calm down. Just calm down. Hal and Pat run around every which way throwing wood on the fire. Goddamnit, why don't they just sit down? The motion makes me dizzy. They're driving me crazy.

The fire is going now, and I lose myself in the flames and billowing smoke. What was that noise? The woods crackle in all directions. Are there people coming? Why didn't we move further back into the woods? It's only squirrels, Pat assures me.

The bottle of orange juice is in my hands. What do I do with this? What is it? I study it until Mel nudges me and tells me to drink. I chug it, and as I drink I think the orange juice is Vodka. Well, I wouldn't know the difference. This is f---- dangerous, man. I'm sweating now. I reach for a cigarette, but can't summon the coordination to take one out of the box.

148

I move from the log to the ground, and as I do so I notice the broken glass lying all around the fireplace. I'm sitting on some. It's all over. I look at a piece. A flick on my wrist and this insanity is over. F---, don't even think that! Hal, what time is it? One? Yeah, I'm peaking. Trips are going around in Iowa that last three days. Jesus, no. Please, no.

Hal has had a revelation, he says, and he babbles incessantly. Half of his words make no sense. I put my head in my hands to try to shut him out. "All human thought," he says, "is merging towards the One Thought, and the body is here to support the Mind in the quest for the Thought; and one day we will all achieve it. Acid helps you all think in unity, do you see?"

"Do you see," T., "do you see?" I look up at him. "When I look in your eyes I see nothing," he says."

"I need to talk to someone," I say.

"You're talking to us," he says.

"Someone who's not tripping, " I say. "I need to talk to Anne. I need reality."

"This is reality," they say.

"Don't say that shit, man. Can't you see I'm going crazy?"

Every second is now an eternity. I need to do something. I stand up. Whoa, man! That worked! It's over. I breathe a sigh of relief. My peak has passed, and it's all downhill from here. I take a piss and sit down by the fire to enjoy what's still running around my system.

As we walk home, the sun fades and twilight sets in. It's six now, but damn, I'm still tripping. As I approach home this worries me. I brace myself for dealing with my family. I eat dinner feeling that all eyes are on me, watching my hand tremble as I struggle to pin down the peas in the fingers of my fork. I excuse myself, and go upstairs.

I call Anne, and she answers on the first ring. Thank God. "Think positive and listen to good music," she says. My voice trembles but her voice soothes. Did I make sense? I ask myself as I hang up the phone.

I take Anne's advice, and listen to music and smoke cigarettes until I finally feel my body getting tired. I lie down to sleep, but when I close my eyes lights dance in my head, and I feel my heart beating faster and louder. I try reading but the words jump around on the pages. I close my eyes. I read, I close my eyes. I read, I close my eyes.

"Tom, " my mom calls. I open my eyes to see the first shades of dawn coloring the sky.

T. O. B.

What's in this memoir? What was in it for you? Does the memoir give you a good sense of what it's like to "trip"? If so, how does he manage this? Should he have stepped out of the story and made some points, or a point? What would that have done to the memoir? Does it feel as if the narrative leans toward a single theme, a particular attitude toward the "trip," or is his perspective complex?

149

The following memoir is a story of one night's training for a company of women on an Army firing range. But it's more than a memoir; within the memoir is an essay.

Night Firing

It's near dusk at Fort McClellan, Alabama, at the end of a hot humid July day. I'm standing on Range 22 as part of the cadre of Company D, Second WAC [Women's Army Corps] Basic Training Battalion. We're here as Safety NCOs to put some two hundred trainees through the M16 rifle night firing orientation. It lets the trainees get a feel for night vision in general, firing the weapon on automatic in specific. They haven't done that before. I remember being through this myself as a trainee in basic training only a little more than a year ago. I can't believe I'm supposed to be a trainer now.

Normally my domain is the company Orderly Room or the battalion headquarters because I'm the Company Clerk. But all training company staff become trainers at one point or another. At least that's what the First Sergeant told me when she said, "Specialist Flynn, time to get your feet wet."

My feet are in formerly shining black boots, which are now covered with fine brown dirt and sand. The starched and pressed fatigues I wear are getting wet from sweat. The range stretches out in front of me from left to right a good half-mile across. Down range, far beyond the twenty-five meter targets, I see rows of green trees. Clouds above them are catching the escaping sunlight in tones of red and orange. I breathe in deeply, smell the trees and sun and earth.

Thirty trainees are on the firing line lying on their bellies with their weapons pointed down range. I know most of them are older than I am and wonder if they can figure out that I'm barely twenty. The fatigues make us all look tough at a distance but my face is smooth and soft and very young looking. All the Drill Sergeants in the company tease me about it, about being the youngest staff member in the entire battalion. Right now some of those Drill Sergeants, working as Safety NCOs with me, are on the line teasing the trainees with comments like, "Don't you be pointing that weapon at me," and, "I better not hear anybody call that thing a gun!"

Working the line on my right is Pat who's only been a Drill Sergeant for five months. Her trainees don't know it and she walks the line as if she's done it for years. Walking her section of the line, Pat checks the body position of each trainee. Occasionally she pauses behind a trainee; the toe of her boot taps the soul of a trainee boot. "Get your body behind that weapon," she says. "Straighten out." Pat looks over my way with a wide, handsome smile and I can't help but smile back. Trainees get crushes on her all the time and she pretends not to notice. But I do. Four weeks ago I sat through hours of listening to her expound on the nomenclature of the M-16 rifle in preparation for her teaching the weapons class. I learned a lot about the M-16. Even more, 1 learned that 1 could listen to Pat talk for hours about anything. Being around Pat gives me a rush of energy, and when I'm afraid of trying something new she says simply, "you can do it," and I believe her.

Down the line to my left is Linda who's training her last platoon before reassignment to Germany. Linda tells me stories about her tour in Vietnam. She was in the WAC Detachment in Long Binh for a year, and she tells me that some women had weapons and could use them. But they weren't issued those weapons and they weren't trained on them. I know this because my basic training class was the first one requiring women to qualify firing the M-16 rifle. "Sometimes," Linda says, "A woman's got to take care of herself."

Further down on the left is Jimmy D. who's only a few years older than I am. He wears the Infantry insignia but hasn't any more experience in life or war than I do.

Way down on the far left of the range is Kathy who wears the Airborne insignia and who is the first female Drill Sergeant in the Army to do so. Kathy jokes about the people who choose to jump out of airplanes; says they've got bird shit for brains so they dont mind falling out of the sky. She personally trains all the trainees bound for Airborne school, and none of them ever fail the final test.

Our Senior Drill, Birch, comes sauntering down the line with an unlit cigarette hanging from his lips. Birch is real Infantry, did two tours in Vietnam and got a Purple Heart to show for it. He says he prefers training women on weapons because women have enough sense to fear them. An Alabama boy, Birch passes me, says, "hey," and winks.

The darkness seems to suddenly clamp down over the horizon an, the range lights flash a white, bright light. We all look as if we're on a movie set. The tower loudspeaker buzzes and whines, then blares in a deep male voice, "Are Range Personnel Ready to Fire?" Each of us on line signals the Training Officer as she walks by. "Is Anyone Down Range?" the tower asks, and my eyes instinctively seek the now black horizon. "Firers, Assume a Good Night Fire Position. Insert One Thirty-Round Magazine and Secure Your Weapon."

I feel my heartbeat kick up a notch as I hear the whacks of ammunition magazines being smacked into rifles. Sweat trickles down my back as I walk from trainee to trainee in my section of five, making sure there are no problems, and wondering what on earth I'll do if there are any. I have to make sure each trainee has the arm of whatever hand is holding the rifle barrel wound through the heavy sling of the weapon, so that the recoil from automatic firing doesn't jerk the barrel skyward—or out of her hand to point back at me. My last trainee has her arm wound through the sling twice, and so tightly it's practically a tourniquet. 1 say, "Whoa, just once through the sling. "I position her arm and hand, notice they're trembling ever so slightly.

"Is the Firing Line Ready?" the tower asks, and I give my signal to the Training Officer. Then the range lights go out.

It's very dark. Very quiet. All of us are still as we wait in the darkness. One hundred and seventy trainees sitting on the ground some twenty feet behind us, waiting to be next, are quiet. Somewhere far away from us is the faint sound of chirping crickets. I look down range and slowly shift my line of vision from left to right and finally pick up the reflectors on the twenty-five meter targets. I hear a snapping noise to my left and look over to see Linda pointing to the ear protectors she's wearing. I pull mine up from around my neck as the tower intones, "Unlock Your Weapons." There's a soft sound of scraping metal up and down the line. It becomes quiet again. We all wait. I'm barely breathing, aware of the humidity, the sweat beading up on my forehead, the hairs of my arms standing up. I cannot believe I'm doing this.

"Commence Firing!" booms the tower, and thundering rifle fire explodes through the night air, rips through the expanse of range. Tracer bullets light up the sky with long, high arcs of light, and I know the firers aren't controlling the rifle barrels. Insistent booming echoes back from the horizon. I yell! "Get that weapon down!" knowing all the Drill Sergeants are shouting likewise. "Hold that sling!" The firers gain control; the arcs of light begin to flatten out as the magazines are expended. The firing sputters and dies, the night sky turning dark again as the tower commands, "Cease Fire! Cease Fire!"

The range lights come up, and my eyes sting from the brightness. Smoke drifts across the horizon like a rally of ghosts. I hear the click-click-click of magazines being disengaged from weapons. The scent of smoke burning in my nose, I move from trainee to trainee making sure each has cleared her weapon, put the safety switch on. I hear, "Lock and Clear All Weapons. Firers Remain in Position Until Cleared by Safety NCOs."

I give my signal to the Training Officer as she moves down the line. Then the tower calls, "The Firing Line is Clear." Two platoon sergeants and a spare Training Officer come hustling down the line to move the trainees off and bring another group on. I see the other Safety NCOs walking away from the line for a minute of break and join them at the base of the tower.

I feel breathless, exhilarated, as if I'd just run down range and back Kathy slaps me on the back. "How are you Flynner?" I smile mutely, stupidly. I think of my parents back home who believe I do nothing in uniform but tap a typewriter.

"Bet were done by twenty-three hundred hours," Linda says as Jimmy D. squints up into the range lights to see what bugs are flying around them. I've been up since 0430 hours and feel as if I could stay out here all night.

Pat wipes the sweat off her forehead with the back of her hand. "Damn it's hot." She catches my eye with a grin. "Say, you look like you belong here."

Birch walks up to us whistling a nondescript tune. "All right, Safety NCOs, let's get them gals firin."

Linda walks with me as we move to the line and she quietly says, "I think I'm going to miss this when I leave." She smiles, playfully pushes me to my own

152

direction, and I step up to the line where my new group of trainees lies. They turn their heads to size me up and I feel the thrill of anticipation run through my body. I gaze up for a moment and see the southern sky filled with the glitter of a million stars. The slightest hint of a breeze picks up and caresses my face as the tower asks, "Is the Firing Line Ready?"

E. Flynn

Until recently men, service men especially, have claimed firearms for themselves. What is the essay suggesting, symbolically? Men have used firearms for hundreds of years to "take care of themselves"—and others. (Guns are also a notorious symbol of male sexuality.) The trainees are all women, as are several of the trainers.   Women's issues are a major subject. How does she present these issues through her memoir/essay? Does she ever step outside her narrative to make points? What is, or would be, the effect?

The author of the following memoir, reviewing her semester's writing, had this to say about the piece. [The memoir itself follows her short note.]

I chose to write about a memory. This I would have to say is my favorite paper. I chose a very painful memory to write about.   I personally feel that the more personal the paper is the more emotion and passion I can put into it. It was kind of easy to write this paper. It was hard to go back to a memory that I have tried to forget for a long time. After re-reading the paper I felt very proud of myself. It took a lot of courage for me to write about this.

It was like any other boring day in my tenth-grade lift. Sitting in class while all of the other girls whisper, and try to get info out of me about my boyfriend, who happens to be a senior. They giggle and make little jealous comments. I have been with Jay for almost a year. Yeah, he's older than I am, but we have so much fun together!
It is finally lunch, and I can get away from these stupid girls in my class. I slowly make and bought me my favorite, a Snapple Iced Tea, and an orange. She's the best.
"What's up, hum?" she asks?
"Nothing really, just the usual!" I say.
"What are you doing after school today?"
"I am going out with Jay," I say.
I love going out with Jay after school! We spend the whole day, or what's left of the day after school, together, laughing and just having fun.
"What are you guys going to do?" Sarah asks as she peels my orange for me. She knows how much I hate to peel them myself.

153

"I think we are just going to go and hang out at his house. Maybe we will go to our spot in the field," I say. Jay and I found this amazing field of wild flowers and all that tall grass that looks like wheat, and it comes up to your waist. We have spent so much time there. We hike in the woods from behind his house to the field; then we follow the beaten path we've made to this area that we have patted down. It looks just like a nest. It's about the size of a blanket; the tall grass and flowers surround you so when you sit you feel like you are in a nest. Grass and flowers all around and nothing but sky above.

Sarah and I continue to talk about how much our school sucks, and how the day is at least halfway over. Jay is lucky because he has senior privilege. That is when you get to leave early, and because he doesn't have any classes, he leaves right before lunch. So he gets to leave for the day and I have to sit in my classes and rot. Lunch is over; Sarah and I slowly walk upstairs to got to our classes.

"Well dude, call me later when you are home from hanging out with Jay. I might go out with my sister for a while, but I will probably be home," she says.

"I will call you, I promise!" We give each other a hug and a kiss, then make our way to our classes.

Finally it is two-thirty! I walk to my locker, and grab my coat and bag. I walk slowly outside to the stone wall where I always sit and wait for Jay to pick me up. I am waiting when Jay's friend, Nick, comes and sits by me.

"What's up, Julie?" he says. "Nothin' much, Nick, just waiting for Jay to come and pick my ass up! How about you?"

"I am just going home, and I saw you sitting here, so I figured I would keep you company until that asshole shows up!" He laughs.

"Jay's not an asshole," I say with a giggle.

"You never know, you better watch it with him . . . I'm just f___ with you!" he says.

I laugh. Finally Jay pulls up, and I say bye to Nick and then hop in the front seat of Jay's car. He and Nick chat through his window, and I don't pay much attention; I just want to leave this awful school and go do something. They finish talking and Nick walks away. Jay turns to me and gives me a big kiss.

"How was the rest of your day?" he asks.

"It was okay," I say. "So what are we going to do today?"

"I figured we could just go to my house and hang out, and maybe go for a walk up to the nest since it's so nice out. Does that sound good to you?"

"Sure, that sounds fine," I say.

We pull into Jay's driveway, get out of the car and walk into his house. We both plop onto the couch and he turns on MTV. We watch it for a while, and then Jay turns and looks at me. "What?!" I say.

"We've been together for almost a year Julie."

"I know that, Jay."

"I just want you to know that I really care a lot about you," he says and gives me a nice soft kiss. I just smile at him.

154

Jay and I have an interesting relationship. We have been together for almost a year, and we haven't had sex. It doesn't seem to bother him. We have talked about it, but he knows I am a virgin, and that I want it to be right. He doesn't rush me into it, and I like that. It makes me believe that he is with me for more than just sexual reasons.

Jay shuts the television off and goes to grab the orange blanket that we always bring with us to the field.

"Let's go for a walk to the nest," he says and grabs my hand.

We walk slowly through the woods until we come to the edge of the field. We then walk along the path that we have beaten down over time. I walk slowly and pick flowers like I always do. I let the heat of the sun warm my back and face. When I get to the nest, Jay has the blanket spread out, and is lying face up. His eyes are closed and he is soaking in the sun.

I sit down next to him and look at the flowers I just picked I pull a daisy out of the bouquet, and rub the soft petals on my cheeks and lips. I put the flower down with the rest and lie down next to Jay. He pulls me close and rests my head on his chest. We lie there in silence for a while, like we usually do.

I look up at the piercing blue sky and search the puffy white clouds for an animal or a shape. I always do that, see if I can see things in the clouds. I lie there and look as a big fluffy sheep starts to form and float across the sky. It seems to hang above us, and I smile as it slowly moves away.

"Julie . . ." Jay breaks the silence.

"Yes . . ."

He sits up and looks at me.

"I need to talk to you about something."

"Ok," I say.

"We have been together for a while now and I know I told you this before, but I really do care about you a lot. I love you Julie!"

My eyes and face begin to burn with excitement and emotion.

"I love you too, Jay," I say.

He smiles at me and pulls me close to him. He gives me a kiss and rubs my back. Then he moves to my neck, and holds me close to him the entire time he is kissing me. He lays me down on the blanket and lifts my shirt revealing my sixteen-year-old stomach, tight and flat with muscle. He moves slowly up my belly kissing me. He lifts up my bra; my young and perky breasts respond to his gentle touch. He kisses me and is now on top of me. I am so nervous that I am shaking.

Jay and I have done all this before, but today I feel it might go farther. He starts to undo my pants.

"Jay," I say with hesitation.

"Are you Ok?" he asks me." Yeah, I just don't know about this."

"I want to make love to you, Julie, trust me; it's OK, I have protection."

"I just don't know if I am ready yet," I say.

155

He pulls my shirt off, and my chest is exposed to the sun's heat. It is burning into me, making me hotter and hotter by the minute. Jay then takes off my pants, and my underwear. I am fully exposed now, lying there naked and nervous as hell. I look up at the sky and search for a shape, or my sheep, to calm me down. But there is nothing but piercing blue sky all around. So I stare up and think to myself, when are you going to be ready, Julie? He loves you and would never hurt you; and you love him too. Would you rather wait and do it with someone who doesn't love or care about you? Or would you rather do it with your boyfriend?

Jay is still kissing my body. He lowers himself on top of me again, and I can feel his heart pounding against mine. He puts his hands on my face, and kisses me. How did he get naked and already put the condom on, I think to myself! I can feel him pressed against me.

"I love you," he says.

"I love you, too."

"Are you ready for this?" he asks.

"Yeah, I think so," I say.

He begins to kiss me again, but this time each kiss is getting less and less gentle. He is pushing himself against me harder, and harder. My body is tense with emotion and nervousness. I look at him and he asks if I am OK. I just nod. Just then I can feel him push himself inside of me. I get a sudden shot of pain shooting through my entire body . . . It stings, and feels hot. He is ripping me apart each time he moves himself in and out of my body. The tears rolls down my cheeks; this is the worst pain I have felt in my entire life. I stare at the blue sky.

"You're OK," he says. At this point I don't know if I am OK anymore. I am in so much pain that I can't imagine that anyone would ever enjoy this. I am being torn and it stings so badly. Each thrust tears me more and more. I am so hot the sun is burning me up. When is this going to be over, I think to myself.

Just then Jay quickens his pace and begins to breathe heavier. Then he is finally done. He kisses me and rolls over onto the blanket. I sit up. My face is stained with tears. I look down; my thighs are covered in blood. I begin to cry again. Jay rolls over and tells me that it is normal for a virgin to bleed, and that the next time it won't hurt so bad.

I lie down and try not to think about the throbbing inside of me. I put all of my clothes back on and sit cross-legged on the blanket. I have my daisies in my hands. I just sit there and stare, wondering when we are going to leave. Jay slowly gets dressed, and we begin to walk back to his house. Every step I take a shooting pain goes through my entire body; I have been torn apart. We get to his house, and I get into the car. He starts the car and drives me back to my house.

"I will call you later on tonight," he says.

"Ok," I say.

I get out of the car and go into my house. I call Sarah but she is not home. So I lie there and cry. I eventually fall asleep in the clothes I have been wearing all day long.

156

My mom wakes me up at six thirty. *I have to get up and get ready for school.*

"Mom, did Jay call last night?"

"No, honey, get ready, we are going to be late."

That's weird, I think, he always calls when he says he will. I get into the shower. I wash the bloodstains off my thighs. The water burns as it hits my cuts and tears. I do not know how I am going to walk, or even go to the bathroom, I think to myself. I get out of the shower and get dressed. I am wearing a cute little skirt; I figured jeans would only rub against me and make it hurt even more. I get into the car and mom drives me to school. She drops me off out front like usual, and I walk inside. I feel like everyone is staring at me. I walk over to Jay to say hi like I usually do. All of his friends start to snicker and laugh.

"Hi," I say.

"Hi Julie." "Why didn't you call me last night, Jay?"

"I forgot to. Listen, I don't think we should see each other any more."

"WHAT!?"

I can feel the tears building up inside of me. I can't believe this is happening. All he wanted was sex from me, and he waited for almost a year, and told me he loved me just to get it. I start to walk away.

"Maybe you shouldn't have bled all over the place," one of his friends says.

"I told you to watch out for him; he's an asshole!" *Nick yells to me as I am walking away.*

"F _you all," I say over my tears with a shaky voice. *I am in the locker trying not to cry as I put my books away. Sarah walks over.*

"Hey hun. What's wrong? Jesus, you look awful," she says.

I grab her and she hugs me. I start to lose it. She leads me into the bathroom. I am crying so hard that I can't speak. She just holds me and tells me everything is going to be Ok. I believe that it is not going to be Ok. "Trust me," he said, and this is what I got. F_ trust. He used me all this time. I should have known better than to trust him.

Julie S.

What sort of voice, and age, does the narrator seem to have? What does the extensive use of dialogue contribute to the memoir? Toward the end there is little dialogue, even though the couple is together. Does that make sense? Are the description and dialogue balanced well with her thoughts? What do her thoughts add to the narration? A number of elements in her description seem symbolic: the beaten path, sun, piercing blue sky, sheep-cloud, nest in the tall grass, and flowers. How do these things connect to the meaning unfolding in the story?

The essay that follows anchors itself to a single happening: a free lunch for employees at the company lunchroom, compliments of the boss, since his employees have just done him the favor of voting the union out. The lunchroom scene is recalled repeatedly. How does it function, especially with regard to theme? The author recalls classic union history, his family history with unions, and his own. What does this do for the theme he is working?

God . . . I feel sick, right to the core of my insides. My guts are churning, it's almost noon; I'll be glad to get out of here. They had a vote today, voted their union representation away, and I want to . . . vomit. It's almost noon, almost quitting time; I can't wait to get away.

They're celebrating in the lunchroom-how could anybody eat? How could anybody smile?

I want to get away, but it's going to stick inside my mind. I think of the Solidarity movement in Poland. I think of Russian coal miners putting it all on the line in the U.S.S.R. I think a lot about what happened to the union men in Germany when the public voted their representation rights away, right after the Nazi party took power.

How could anybody smile!

I know, times have changed! But it's really very personal with me! Besides, I know a fascist when I see one. The owner here is smiling, patting everyone on the back, bought everyone pizza. (Hell of a cheap payoff) A slice of pizza in exchange for a hundred years of struggle. When the owner is done with his lunch, they will all go back to their stations thinking what a great guy the boss is. He will go back to his office and continue the attack

Sonofabitch! The owner will go to his two-million dollar home tonight and congratulate himself on his coup.

How could anybody eat!

He will go home and continue his attack. First will come wages: "Must come down, got to stay competitive. No more of this cradle to grave insurance coverage. Cut back the vacation time; takes the edge off the work force. Must enforce compulsory overtime; gotta get the product out."

It's personal with me!

Dad was a union man. His father and his brother were union men too, Western Mine Workers. They struck in 1922 for mine safety and an eight-hour day. The company brought in scabs, German veterans from the war to end all wars. They brought guns; but the union men brought guns and axe handles. They met the scabs at the railway depot in Wilton, North Dakota, and put the Fascist scum back on the train, sent the sons-of-bitches straight back to Berlin.

After a year they won the strike, held fast, never backed down, lived the meaning of solidarity. They got their eight-hour day, and some improvements in the mine. It didn't cure grandpa's black lung, dad still had to do his eight hours in the hole, after school. They had to make ends meet; times were still hard. They had to put

158

dinner on the table, and buy enough coal to stoke the furnace against the North Dakota winter, but they were making headway.

A God damned lunch of pizza—a smile-a pat on the back! How could anybody eat?

Had my own history with the union. It's personal with me. I worked in union shops for nearly twenty years. I've been on strike nearly as many months. Nothing nearly as rough as dad and grandpa went through. The union had become strong by then so we played down the adversary role. Became civilized, thought the boss was civilized too. Then he locked the door. Moved to Mexico where the autoworkers work for nearly nothing.

How could anybody smile!

I got by all right; I'm married to a good woman with a profession. Got good kids, too. We were very fortunate; you might say blessed, if you lean towards religion. I watched, for as long as I could, my fellow workers decline. A lot of alcoholism. Families broke up. Folks moved away to God knows where. And every now and then there'd be a suicide. Union carried us long as they could, almost two years. A hundred dollars a week and paid our insurance. I got no complaint!! They treated us well. The boss, he's in Mexico, being civilized to his new help.

I work part time here now; I didn't qualify to be in the union, to vote. Doesn't matter much after today. The employees voted their union out.

I think about Solidarity in Poland, the miners in the U.S.S.R holding fast to what they knew. I think about what happened in Berlin some sixty years ago. Mostly I think about grandpa and pa, the strength and dignity they had.

They're celebrating in the lunchroom; they voted the union out. They're all smiling and eating pizza.

Bruce MacMartin

How does Bruce's repeated return to the lunch room scene work for this piece? Is this a statement of theme? If so, how direct, or indirect, is it? Does Bruce ever step outside the story to state his theme? If so, what would that have done (or did it do) to the "voice" evident in his essay? Bruce goes beyond his immediate experience to sketch his family history and to refer to incidents in the history of unions. What do these histories contribute to his theme?

APPENDICES

A Short Summary of Basics, Experiential Writing

1. If it is to have life, writing needs to sound like talk, actual talk, or the way inner talk sounds. That is, writing should capture the mind's movement with experience, the movement of feeling.

> *"Six bucks," she said again. I never saw her before. Didn't order any cookies either. She just kept her hand out. "Six bucks." I gave her the money.*

2. Writing that follows feeling wastes no words.

> *Ninety-pound people who are wrinkled with age, lying on their sides and perhaps half off the bed, in that position for hours and sometimes days. Some of them weeping softly to themselves, others lying with such apathy. I am full of disgust. Lethargic and weak, fearing everyone they meet. My stomach just churns.*

3. In order to "make sense" writing must capture the sense of experience in concrete, descriptive details.

> *Slowly, laboriously, she shaves my enormous belly. The water on the razor is ice cold and I flinch with each stroke.*

A simple rule applies to capturing the sense of experience: You must be able to feel, taste, smell, hear, and see the experience—in its specifics—with whichever of these five senses your mind is making its capture. Hearing includes the descriptiveness of "voice."

4. Description is symbolic, carrying likenesses to an intangible, human situation "close to home."

> *Suddenly I feel this shocking pain in my hands. I look at my hands and they're covered with a red liquid. My blood! As I look closer, I notice they are two ferrets. I try to shake them lose but their teeth are deeply embedded in my skin. Nothing I try will break them loose.*

160

5. Within its symbolic sense of experience the mind usually suggests a dominant metaphor, a *prominent* likeness to the experience. This metaphor can remain implied within the image, or be made explicit, that is, stated.

...my two "pesty" bosses give me "sharp pain," and I can't seem to shake it; they've got too much of a "bite" on me! My innocent space is now covered with the best of me—my life . . .

The mind urges an explicit *statement of meaning* when you need to grasp the situation, take a stance with regard to it—and act.

Punctuation, Especially as it Relates to "Voice"

Marks of punctuation can be seen as devices to control "voice," especially its pace, rhythm, and accent. Though many "rules" (usage agreed upon) govern all sorts of special situations, a good share of punctuation can follow your sense of pauses or breaks in the flow of words. (See end note.) For the "rules," and agreed upon usages for all sorts of special cases, check the punctuation section of your dictionary, or a handbook of English. In the meantime, here's a short version of punctuation primarily related to "voice."

The Period is the most common means of indicating a *full stop* in voice (as the British say). The voice drops, and stops. Generally a statement has been made. Another will follow. Making a statement is an important act. A human being has stepped into the picture and *said* something. Period. Oh yes, sentence fragments can have the same effect, though the statement is only implied. The period gives them the weight of a complete sentence, the statement understood.

The Semicolon marks off statements just as a period does, but it indicates that the statements are closely related; it *flags* that relationship, as in this sentence where I've got two closely related statements. The semicolon's pause is almost as long as the period's, but it's not so definite; something more is to come.

You will, at times, find that you've simply put a *comma* between two *statements*, it won't do, as you can see in the sentence you are now reading. The comma before "it won't do" doesn't mark that statement as a separate statement, doesn't suggest its importance. The comma pause isn't enough to flag two *statements*. Notice what happens when a semicolon is replaced by a comma

The firers gain control, the arcs of light begin to flatten out as the magazines are expended.

A semicolon between "control" and "the arcs" (her original) would flag the two *statements* and give us the pause needed between two statements.

The semicolon also indicates a major division in long, complex sentence, such as the one below.

The Greek howls with laughter, roars till tears come down his face, till he's choking on cigar smoke, till the whole damned table is laughing with him, pounding fists, hands, bottles, laughing and laughing; and I'm laughing right with them.

Here the semicolon marks off *their* laughter and *hers*; simply adding another comma after "laughing" would not clearly mark the major division in the sentence.

162

A Colon is a sit-up-and-take-notice mark that is essentially an equals (=) mark. It says this: everything following the colon will equal what was said or was indicated would be said before the colon, as in this sentence.

"Dear John:" says that a letter is to be written. "Let me make three points:" says that three points are coming. "This is what she said:" says rather definitely that words of hers will follow.

The Comma is the most common mark to indicate pause, generally a brief pause, as you see here. The previous sentence also indicates another common use of the comma, marking *two* pauses that set off a phrase within the main sentence, what's often called, rather strangely, a "parenthetical phrase." You've just seen a second parenthetical phrase in the previous sentence.

One kind of parenthetical word or phrase, usually short, simply identifies, names, or defines what comes before (called, anciently, an "appositive").

At last, I could feel him, <u>my son</u>, *sliding through this artificial opening, his head, shoulders, hands, body, legs, feet.*

"My son," identifies "him."

Commas used for the list in the entry above (head, shoulders, etc.) illustrate another very common use for commas, marking the items of a list. Usually an "and" precedes the last item. What feel does the absence of "and" give in the entry above?

One more common use of the comma is to indicate words left out, that is, assumed silently to be there. In the last sentence, between "that is" and "implied," you should have mentally supplied "words."

Dashes and Parentheses carve out a phrase or statement from a sentence, but with opposite effects. Parentheses *de*-emphasize whatever they carve out (you can see that here); they often give that phrase or statement a different voice (can you tell?). But dashes usually *emphasize*—by typographically breaking the sentence. Look again.

Fast Tom makes his move and—whap!

Would he rather live with the pain and the people he loved or give it all up— nobody asked him . . . Never—never will he see his kids smile or feel his wife's arms around him or complain about the weather or taxes . . .

Ellipses (. . .) indicate a pause that has two related functions: It indicates that something is missing in the sentence; and it gives the reader a little time to think . . . perhaps about what is missing, as in this and the following sentence, which

163

comes at the end of a long journal entry about a boyfriend the writer has made into a fantasy You. All through the entry she's fighting to reconcile the real and fantasy person.

> *I thought I could make You do as I want, flatter Me the right way, make Me a happy person—you're a person . . . those qualities I left out when I formed You.*

Ellen Moore

Quotation Marks ("") are easily forgotten, but are important to indicate someone's exact words. That's easy enough. And where you have a *new* speaker you need a new paragraph (even for one word), to indicate the change; a different person is being introduced. This is simply to avoid the confusion of speakers. (Professional writers will ignore this rule, especially when the dialogue needs to run swiftly.)

> *One of the team members asks me a question. I reiterate his question and add my own; "where is my husband?"*
> *"Can you feel this?" Again he says this.*
> *"Where is my husband?"*

> *"Cam I hab a cap'm am coke, pleez Jem?" "Are you driving, Baby?" "I'm mot. Mai carr iz." "Wrong answer!"*

If you have a long quote covering more than one paragraph, don't end the paragraph with a quote mark; your reader will think that you're done quoting. Start the new paragraph with a quote mark: you're still quoting.

John Dawkins (mentioned at the end of Chapter 1) has presented a model of punctuation that fits perfectly with punctuation as it relates to "voice." Punctuation should be used for emphasis, as short to long pauses in speaking do. He sees the various marks of punctuation in a hierarchy that uses pauses to indicate more emphasis, or less. A period, question mark, or exclamation mark give maximum emphasis. A semicolon, colon and dash give medium emphasis—though a dash is an emphatic mark. A comma gives minimum emphasis. With no punctuation there's no emphasis (CCC 46/December 1995, p. 535).

Punctuation for emphasis operates without strict observance of the rules. A comma can separate two short statements. Though a semicolon usually separates two statements, it can simply mark a longer pause, an important divide, within a long, complex sentence; this sentence, for example, which might not indicate its two main parts if only commas were used. A period usually marks off a "complete statement." But, as you've seen throughout the book, it's quite useful to mark off sentence fragments. For emphasis, as professional writers do.

164

CPSIA information can be obtained
at www.ICGtesting.com
Printed in the USA
LVHW081942061220
673493LV00015B/1753